BERT'S LAW

by Bert Gibson

Acknowledgement

My grateful thanks go to my friend Gordon Wilkinson who, despite his obvious pain and suffering, chose to stand by me to the last page Thanks Gordon.

Chapter One

Fourteen years as a copper in the Northumbria Police had come and gone. Now, 34 years of age, I would work among the intellectuals as a trainee solicitor putting in 50 hours a week, called out during the night and weekends to police stations, but I was happy. Just like winning the national lottery, but I had achieved my ultimate goal of qualifying as a solicitor. An enormous leap of faith by an ex copper, an intellectual lightweight, with two active children who demanded my attention every spare moment. It would not be easy but I was up for the challenge and determined to give it my best shot; my family and our future depended on it.

January 1980. Road`s icy, snow lying thick in the fields. At 3 a.m. and I answered a call from the West End Police Station. "Got one in custody asking for your attendance."

Half asleep, I rolled out of bed, fastened up my overcoat and slid my way through the slush in my car, the streets virgin white and silent.

The detainee, a man in his thirties, was lounging in his cell calm and unfazed his eyes half closed his back propped against the cold wall and thick nicotine fingers meshed above his head as if settling in for the night. "Your client has been arrested for stealing fifteen live chickens," the Custody Sergeant told me with a poker face and that I knew was the moment I would remember for many years to come.

The cell door swung open and I wandered inside to introduce myself. "The copper told me the chickens were not mine." He growled. "The copper said they belong to someone else… but they are definitely mine," he insisted, although unable to remember where or how he got them. My suspicion`s as an ex copper were raised. The law requires the police to present hard evidence and as far as I could remember chickens cannot talk. The interview began in earnest, the officer leaning in close, eyeball to eyeball to my client, insisting he had stolen them. "Prove it copper." He sat back with an arrogant smirk and the copper dug his heels in certain he could prove the theft and a conviction would soon follow. I made notes of their exchanges, "You did…no I did not"

"You stole them…" The Officer insisted.

"Did not" The questions repetitious and going nowhere.

I asked the question: "How can you prove who owns the chickens? Did they tell you they were stolen?" Sarcastic yes, but I was tired and it was freezing cold. At 9:00a.m, I had places to go and people to see.

"How can you identify a chicken?" A brilliant leading question I thought

"We recovered them from his garden shed." He bragged.

"And how are you able to tell one chicken from another?" I raised a questionable eyebrow, "Are they ringed… like pigeons, or a rare breed?"

"I was present when the owner identified all fifteen."

"…and how did he do that?" I was dying to know.

"He shouted to them all… `Looby Loo`…and they came running." Is this a wind up? I wondered. Are we on Candid Camera? From then on the interview went down- hill until another officer intervened, deciding the chickens would not be able to give evidence against my client and he was free to go home.

*

Being an Articled Clerk was hard work, but fun. I enjoyed visits to prisons, police stations and making nervous applications to a Crown Court Judge in his private chambers.

The firm's senior partner, Mr Beecham, sent me off to Sunderland hospital where a young man lay gravely ill in intensive care, hooked- up to anything with a dial, monitoring the erratic beat of his failing heart. He only had hours to live.

"We can do nothing for him," the medical expert confirmed as nurses hovered at the bedside trying to make his last hours comfortable.

"No magic potion can save his life," the doctor said in a tone of defeat. "It is only a question of time."

I read the incident report. The circumstances were avoidable. He was one of a dozen men employed by the local council to work in the community parks. It was a scorching hot day as they laboured bare-chested, cutting lawns, trimming hedges, sweat pouring and peeling skin. Meal break saw them rushing into the prefabricated hut, demolishing sandwiches and sinking cool drinks with parched lips. He spotted an open pop bottle standing near the door and, in a split second, he had it to his lips. The Foreman leaped to snatch the bottle away, but too late to stop him swallowing the smallest amount.

The pop bottle contained paraquat, the deadliest of poisons and with no known specific antidote, death usually following within a few days.

There would be a substantial claim in damages but that would not help this young man or his grieving parents.

*

I registered with the Law Society to sit my solicitor finals but my application was late and the local centres full. I would have to travel 300 miles to the Alexandra Palace in London.

Eric Lee granted me a few days off to study. I needed it. He wanted to give me the best shot at passing first time, but it would be hard. January rolled around with splashes of snow and dark heavy clouds. My wife Anne dropped me off at Newcastle Central Railway Station and I caught the Edinburgh to London express to Kings Cross, then took the underground train to Seven Sisters Road, trawling for a cheap, B&B.

Darkness was closing the day when I finally knocked on a door with a `vacancy` sign. As luck would have it I managed to book into the worst, the smelliest, the most abhorrent, B&B I could ever have the misfortune to rest my miserable head in. Reminding myself that beggars could not be choosers and it would only be for one night.

A portly man, oily skinned, his belly hanging over a broad leather belt greeted me at the door in a foreign tongue and a grovelling, fawning smile. He led me into a small room at the end of a dark corridor where I studied the single bed, the wardrobe and a stained side table with a flowery lamp on top.

"The last room" he praised my good fortune, his hand's outstretched enveloping my cash. I reached for my handkerchief pressing it against my nose: curry and rotting vegetables lingering in the air. It was only for one night. I closed the door and flopped recklessly onto the bed, surveying my surroundings. I would be counting the hours until I departed.

I drew the curtains, pulled back the blanket and jumped into bed. I reached for my haversack and my well- fingered textbooks, flicking through the pages. Tomorrow would be a career changing opportunity.

It was only 11:00 p.m. but I felt I had spent a week in that room, my eyelid's drooping and the blustery wind blowing up a storm against the bedroom window. I ducked under the cover and snuggled down for the night.

Then my alarm clock screamed out a warning to get up and face the new day.

The blanket wrapped tightly around my shoulders I stepped to the window and wiped away the condensation on the glass. The Seven Sisters Road and the old Victorian rooftops opposite covered in a blanket of snow. There was silence. It seemed all of the City of London had come to a grinding halt. Not a car, bus or lorry trundled passed along this busy route into London and the footpath, and the road a hundred metres to my left and right, painted silky white.

A radio broadcast from the room next door broke the silence with a warning of roads closed and public transport cancelled. How would I get to my destination?

I threw off my blanket and quickly dressed, gathering my books and slung my haversack over my shoulder heading for the door but, just two steps down the path I slipped and fell on my backside.

These shoes would not do. I picked my way along Seven Sisters Road, heading for the underground, joining the gathering crowds with every step. I asked the time. "Its blaady eight firtee five mite" was the rattled response from a cockney accent. I nodded my thanks and pressed forward, reaching for a lamppost or the wing mirror of a parked car to help keep me upright. Stepping warily, unable to tell where the footpath ended, and the road began. Just over an hour to the exams.

A scream of distress filled the air and I turned to see a woman falling and landing with sickening thud, her arms her legs thrashing. Two men rushed to her aid. I looked on as she was lifted gently onto her feet none the worse.

I slipped and slid along to the underground, picking my way down the steps and onto to the crowded platform where anxious people jostled for poll position, squeezing my way through, chest to chest, eyeball to eyeball to the platform edge, the swirling crowds hissing abusively at my behaviour.

"The next train will be 18 minutes late," a voice rang out over the loudspeaker…"and, due to the weather conditions there will be no more trains running before mid-afternoon." The speaker clicked off and the swell of bodies lurched forward in one synchronised step.

I was head and shoulder above most. I glanced around, taking in the easiest route with steely determination to be on this last train… or die. Chivalry, courtesy and honour were yesterday`s words. This was war.

Inch by inch, like an SAS soldier I plotted my foray towards the platform, leaning on the weak and the infirm. "I`m gonna` be on that bloody train."

I heard the train rumbling then a biting blast of freezing cold wind stirring from the tunnel as it shunted laboriously into the station, its brake`s squealing and anxious voices raised.

"Keep clear of the doors please," the announcer called out as the doors swished open. The rush was on with squealing cries and curses filling the air; expletives reserved for a battlefield. Bitter moans and groans, and arms outstretched, grasping at the safety bars inside, pulling with all their might, twenty or more squeezing into a gap meant only for five.

A hip, a leg pushed inside and with total disregard for others in the certain knowledge that the rest of their anatomy must surely follow. Packed in like sardines. Some young men prepared to climbed onto the parcel-rack rather than miss this train.

"Mind the doors please." The doors swished ready to close as I heaved my frame inside to the howling annoyance of those inside. I grabbed a brass pole and held on and to hell with cockney protests, my rucksack planted firmly between my knees.

I allowed myself a smile, glancing along the carriage, saluting the victorious few, the chosen ones who had fought the good fight, and now on board. Strained, flushed faces, gnashing teeth, coiffured dangling hair. The train rumbled forward.

A smart young woman, her handbag gripped between her teeth, tried to free up one arm to check the time. I gave her a congratulatory smile but in return received a harsh, condescending stare, her head turning away sharply with an expression of disgust. I did not care. I was on my way to the Alley Pally and I smiled the smile of a winner. Nothing else mattered. 9:12 a.m. and I began to panic. I still had a twenty- minute walk up a steep hill to the venue.

I was willing the doors to open, counting the seconds as the train pulled to a halt. We poured out, almost horizontally, onto the wet platform. A battalion of law students stampeding up the escalator, into the snow and biting winds, marching, like a well-drilled army, along slippery pathways, some on knees reaching out for fences, rails, tree branches and anything capable of offering them progress. We stepped, and slithered inch by inch up to the Alexandra Palace.

Gasps of delight and whispers of thanks to God spread across a broad smile as the splendour of the building loomed ahead, spurring me on, and into a hall bigger than an aircraft-hanger, decked out with rows and rows of desks. I estimated fifty or more rows wide and one hundred deep, running off into the distance. Reference number in my hand I set off, at double pace, in search of my desk, swerving through alleyways, zigzagging between desks, then dropping exhausted, onto my seat. It felt good. A heavy weight lifted off my shoulders then a moment of calm, the trauma of the occasion sinking in.

Several angry pigeons perched high on the rafter ranted noisily, marching like indignant Hitler`s, flapping furious wings in protest at this uninvited invasion of their domain. A dollop of shit dropped from one like a guided missile, splattering on the floor near to my feet. Was this a sign of good luck? Did it mean I would pass the exams? Stupid questions, I was losing the plot.

A continuous flow of students rushed passed their faces pale and dizzy expressions, leaping like gazelles from row to row and collapsing onto cold seats. I emptied my haversack of pens and pencils and nearly skewered my left eye in the process. Nerves were getting the better of me.

A loud squeal and a chair dragged across a polished floor drew my attention to a young girl fainting. She dropped like a felled tree and lay semi- conscious, moaning. I was ready to rush to her aid but decided to let the invigilators take charge. Time to start was drawing near.

"Now here this, now here this," a voice of authority called out over the loudspeaker, his voice echoing around the hall and disappearing into the roof: "you must not turn over your examination papers until I tell you." The microphone gave a rasping high-pitched squeal and several pigeons took flight, swooping low across our heads almost in combat fashion then settling onto a wide frosty window ledge.

"You may begin."

I blew into my hands and reached for my pen. The temperature was only a degree or two warmer than outside. I nervously turned the pages of the booklet, praying for easy questions. Questions I had studied. The battle to become a solicitor had begun and in the next three hours, maybe less, it would be over… unless it wasn`t.

Twenty minutes past and students still rolled inside their shoulders rounded, exhausted expressions and leaping to find their seat, eye's tearful at the thought of the precious time lost.

The unforgiving clock ticked on and then the doors locked. Students still outside, stragglers with their faces pressed against the glass and fist's thumping, would be denied access. Pleadings ignored no sympathy shown.

"You are too late," the invigilator shouted: "You will have to register again to take the exams." Another year lost. The harsh weather, the freezing cold, ice and thick snow, matters entirely out of our control would put back their legal career.

I thought about their unfortunate predicament…but only for a moment. 'Sod them, we all have problems and that was theirs'

I filled the pages with every morsel of law that came to mind, relevant or not, scribbling furiously every piece of learning that popped into my dizzy head searching for the best answer, until my head ached and my fingers pained.

Only twenty- five minutes to go. I sat back exhausted, mind now empty, my shoulder's stiff and rounded. I could do no more. That was it. I closed the booklet and took off, grabbing my haversack and headed for the door. The midday sun shone high, the highways full of heavy traffic. In those few hours London had come alive.

I made my way back down the hill, my thoughts full of possibilities. Had I passed? Would I have to re-sit? Running through answers missed, I headed for Kings Cross Station.

It was 12:45 pm I wandered into Kings Cross Railway Station a giddy, unrealistic, feeling of success planted in my mind then searched the list of train departures, heading to the platform and stopping on route for a sandwich and a couple of Mars Bars for the journey back to Geordie land.

A comfortable seat, a four hour journey and the trauma of the day, yesterday's news.

I scrambled on board, second class as a posh- voice spoke over the tannoy, "We apologies, but the train to Edinburgh will depart forty minutes late as the points are frozen," her voice drifting as if submerged under water, she continued: "There will be no heating on the carriages. No hot food or drinks served. We apologise for the inconvenience." The speaker clicked off and I cursed inwardly at the delay.

I stacked my haversack then made myself comfortable looking on with disinterest as seat`s filled to capacity. Men hiding behind newspapers, mother`s clucking over boisterous children, computer`s tapping rhythmically.

A whistle blew followed by a loud clank and we were moving. The train shunted slowly forward. It was 2: 0`clock by my watch and already an aged Railway Inspector, long, lean and well past his sell by date was checking passenger tickets and calling out the latest information of our journey.

"Point`s frozen," he repeated each time he punched a hole in a ticket: "A Line Ganger with burning equipment is walking in front of the train, unfreezing each set of points" he kept apologising.

This journey was going to be long, very long.

It took ten minutes to clear the Station, another twenty minutes to rumble half a mile north on squeaking railway lines at 10 miles per hour, children running amok, storming the isles and refusing to obey demented parents. Trains should have seat belts, I ventured.

Out into the countryside the scenery bright and beautiful with long flowing, drifting snow covering undulating fields near and far and swathed in glistening, sparkling diamonds as the rays of the sun caught the tree-tops. The train struggled on.

"No. Steven. Put that down," a young mother called out objectionably as she set off in pursuit of her troublesome son. "Can you please come back here and sit down, please, just for a few minutes." She shouted too near to my ear. I picked up an abandoned newspaper and hid, praying the journey would pass quickly, but, as shit happens, it turned out to be the longest, the most miserable journey of my entire life.

9:30p.m, seven and a half hours later with nothing hot to drink or eat, the sun gone, my bum sore and sick of my life. It had been a long day. I had read everything within view and, thank God, children were subdued with heads pressed deep in mothers breasts.

We shunted into York Station. My nose pressed against the window and the train, blowing steam out of a knackered engine.

The train came to a halt on platform 10. Silence reigned. I stuck my face to the frosted window and peered out in search of a sign for hot food and warmth. I saw an open fire burning in the waiting room and stretched out my arms, wishing I could cook my backside on it and contemplating the rest of the journey: Darlington, Durham then Newcastle Central. For me just a short hop left, but many passengers, including exhausted children, were heading to Edinburgh.

A call came over the loudspeaker: "The train now standing at platform 10 will be delayed for forty five minutes while a replacement engine is attached. Those wishing to transfer onto the train now standing on platform 12, for Edinburgh, stopping at Darlington, Durham and Newcastle should board now as it will depart in five minutes."

A burst of activity, like a nuclear explosion, saw carriage doors fly open as hundreds of passengers leapt out, suitcases banging and dragging screaming kids. Hot food and a warm train awaited us on Platform 12.

I was out like a shot from a gun, striding across to platform 12 and diving into a comfortable seat then watching as the crawlers dragged heavy luggage aboard, searching frantically for a seat, some having to settle in the corridors or inside a vacant toilet. I threw my jacket onto the rack and settled down for a cosy nap.

The loudspeaker broke the silence once more, "The train now standing at platform 12 is about to depart." "Hurrah!" There was a loud cheer then silent astonishment as we looked back to platform 10 and our train departing.

Confused expressions turned to anxious betrayal as our train departed north... then, a long silence when the loudspeaker announced; "Oh dear. We apologise for our error. We got the platform numbers mixed up," there was a guilty cough: "It was the train on platform 10 that was leaving in five minutes. Not platform 12…sorry."

A tumultuous roar of anger spread throughout the carriages as doors flew open and passengers leapt out in search of any one in a railway uniform, intent on hanging him from the nearest lamppost.

Platform 12 was awash with angry people in pursuit of someone, anyone, to blame. A uniform appeared at the top of the railway bridge and, even from my position, I could see fear in his eyes as he disappeared behind a door marked: `Staff Only`

It was another hour before our train departed and 2: O`clock in the morning, 13 hours since departing from Kings Cross, that I stepped off the train, shouldering my haversack and wandering through the Portico for a taxi and my final journey home.

9:30am, the following morning and I was hunched over my desk, ploughing through a pile of files and preparing cases for the Crown Court; yesterday only a memory.

Chapter Two

Monday morning, early January, wet cold and miserable. I shook the dribbles off my umbrella and pushed the reception door open, heading up stairs to my monastic cell on the fourth floor, a room no bigger than a Police Box, its crooked walls, cracked ceiling, a stained desk my new home. For obvious reasons I was not allowed to interview criminal clients up there. They would probably pinch the toilet roll and copper off the roof. 'My little piece of Geordie land' I called it, a few square metres hidden away in the rafters, but I was proud to be an important, though a junior part, of Alan Henderson, Beecham and Lee solicitors 4, Collingwood Street, Newcastle upon Tyne.

Alan Henderson, now retired, had held the prestigious Office of H M Coroner for Newcastle upon Tyne. He occasionally popped into the office to chat and story has it that he had a burning ambition to own a Rolls Royce motorcar. Now, in the autumn of his years, he had fulfilled his desire and a Rolls Royce stood proudly at the office door but, alas, he confessed, he would now have to move house: "it will not fit into my garage."

Jeremy Beecham, the incumbent senior partner, and Leader of the City Council would one day, be honoured with a knighthood. Eric Lee, a well- respected criminal lawyer had agreed to take on the arduous task of honing my skills as an advocate and, eventually, hoped to help him in the courts. Norman Peacock, the third partner, set his expertise in the fields of family and Industrial law. A competent advocate, and a keen eye for business, he would steer the firm on to greater things, his presence instilling confidence in the staff.

My first few days of Articles, which now seems so long ago, was to prepare a Change of Name by deed and, having completed the task, successfully, was thereafter elected and delegated to the exalted position of Change of Name by Deed expert, with all work of a similar nature channelled onto on my desk.

I bounded up the stairs heading to my room on the fourth floor, my light-weight mac flapping like a toreador's cape in my wake then onto the second floor where Jean Barber, Eric's secretary, brought my progress to a sudden halt thrusting a bundle of papers under my arm and firing off instructions. "Eric wants you to go to North Shields Magistrates' Court. Mr Turnbull is sitting in reception. He wants to take out a private summons." Her raised eyebrow told me I was about to do something for which I had neither experience nor qualification.

"Eric should be doing this," she tut, locking my arm around the papers: "Neighbour dispute," she said straightening my kipper tie; "Mr Turnbull cut down a neighbour's tree and the neighbour struck him a good one across his face with a tree branch," she thought it so funny, old men duelling on the garden lawn with tree branches. "You should see Mr Turnbull's face" she smirked, "he has a large bruise covering the whole of his cheek." She disappeared into her office and I retraced my steps to reception, my mind on more mercenary matters such as petrol expenses. The gauge on my battered VW had been blinking on empty since passing Kenton Bar and crying out for sustenance or it would refuse to take me back home. I made a mental note to sweetheart accounts when I got back. I introduced myself to the only man with a crimson face: "That's a nasty bruise," I said giving a doctor's "tut" and closely examining a large weal covering the left side of his cheek.

"I believe it is an Elm?" Mr Turnbull didn't see the joke.

"Did your neighbour do that?" I asked, knowing the answer. He made a sorrowful nod and an ever-so-sorry expression, but to my huge delight, he confirmed he had a Mercedes parked outside. We would travel to the Magistrates' Court at Howard Street in style. By the time we arrived at the court house I knew the whole history of the incident and even what he had for breakfast.

There had been an on-going dispute regarding tree branches hanging over his garden fence, barring the sunset on balmy summer evenings and casting dark shadows onto his patio. "Couldn't enjoy a Gin and Tonic with my wife," he griped, admitting his temper finally snapped and off he went in search of a chainsaw and, several brash strokes later, branches lay scattered everywhere. Incandescent with rage and furious at the wanton destruction of his tree, his neighbour leapt over the fence with much sparring and swishing of tree branches. Mr Turnbull lowered his guard in a counter offensive and lashed across his face.

As soon as we walked into the court I recognised the usher, an ex- copper who, in the early 1960's regularly held sway directing traffic outside of the Spanish City on Rainbow Corner, Whitley Bay. I used to watch him in action, almost a work of art to see him in control. I had personally experienced the traffic flowing on Rainbow Corner and found myself staving off near fatal accidents.

The Usher acknowledged me with a nod, scribbling something down on his clipboard then asking us to take a seat in the waiting room. "I will get to you soon," he said and, within minutes, Mr Turnbull and I pushed into court where a Bench of Magistrates' waited.

Mr. Weightman, the court clerk, shuffled papers then directed me to proceed.

"Put Mr Turnbull into the witness box and take him through his evidence," He said in business tones. I tried to explain I was not a qualified solicitor and had no authority to speak in court or conduct proceedings, but before I could utter a word, I found myself standing in the middle of the room with inquisitive eyes urging me to get on with it.

I hesitated. Big mistake, as Weightman's tone changed: "Put your client in the witness box and take him through his evidence, PLEASE" his voice rising in annoyance. I nervously coughed, pointing Mr Turnbull to the Witness Stand and pressed the Holy Bible in his hand. "Read the oath," I asked, grateful I had some knowledge of Court procedure.

"Err…tell the Magistrates' what happened to you Mr Turnbull," and in very short time the chairman's gavel struck hard on the desk and a private summons was issued, ordering his neighbour to appear before them… on due date; 'to show cause why he should not be Bound over to Keep the Peace and be of good behaviour'.

It was over in the blink of an eye, but I flew from the court in the certain knowledge that I maybe struck off the Roll of Solicitors before I had the opportunity to get on it.

The weeks following and I hid away in my monastic cell, deep in a variety of files and listening to pigeons scrambling over roof tiles. I drove Eric to the courts: mostly Newcastle, Hexham, Gateshead, Chester-Le-Street and as far south as Durham but it was rare for Eric's client's to wander north to Berwick-On-Tweed but, as luck would have it, one sunny Wednesday morning we were cruising up the A1 and crossing the Royal Bridge in to Berwick. We turned into Church Street where the court occupied the upper portion of the Police Station and parked up.

I could smell the fresh sea air. Berwick had been my home in the 1960's and the memories came flooding back of pounding the streets in my police uniform, seeing men in skirts (kilts) wandering through the town with what looked like cows udders dangling between their tree trunk legs and giving my evidence to the court.

The dark oak adorning the walls, the ancient Coat of Arms and the elevated chairs reserved for the privileged few charged with the duty of dispensing the Queen's justice.

The Usher broke the silence with a call to, "all rise;" searching the public gallery for anyone contemptuously to disobey the majesty of the occasion. The magistrates' wandered in, bowing regally to the assembled lawyers then dropping nobly into their cushioned seats ready for the business of the day to begin.

The Chairman cast an eye my way and I could see his doubtful expression: "where have I seen you before? Have I sent you to prison? Then a spark of recognition, a half smile and a kindly nod of acknowledgement, then the first case of the day called on.

Bowing humbly I departed the building leaving Eric to his advocacy and took myself off to walk the walk of happy memories. The Bastions and Peebles, the Kings Own Scottish Boarders, Dewars Lane and the immortal plaque of J.S. Lowry, the famous matchstick painter, pausing at the ancient Russian Cannon pointing menacingly out across the roaring North Sea and wondering: `are we still at war with Russia?`

By mid- afternoon, the business of the day complete, Eric and I headed back to the great city.

The following days I attended police stations, night and day, visited clients ensconced in Durham Prison, prepared briefs for barristers and dropped them into Chambers and a chat with their Clerks. I took trips south of the Tyne to the County of the Three Bishops, taking the opportunity to visit the antique shops and racking up much-needed travelling expenses.

H. M Durham Prison holds prisoners, convicted and on remand awaiting trial. A high-risk prison holding convicted murderers, rapists and robbers. Entry into the prison is via the main arched gates next to Durham Crown Court and, a glance upwards reveals the gallows, the 19th century emblem of execution. As I stepped inside, I often visualised the scene of the condemned man, his hands bound and struggling for his last breath as the rope tightened around his neck, his body swinging limply in the breeze. To this day, I cannot understand why Albert Pierepoint, the official executioner, would want to do such work. How he could sleep at night or reconcile his mind. It is said, he could peek through a gap in the cell door and instantly calculate the height and weight of the prisoner and the length of rope needed to end his life.

Passing through security, we visitor`s are escorted up a flight of stairs and into a room no bigger than a cupboard, the smell of antiseptic filling the air. The temperature inside raised almost to gasping level to make the inmates more listless and less likely to fight… with each other or prison staff.

My client, a lean twenty six year old, was waiting. The magistrates` had remanded him the previous day and he was anxious to discuss his case of burglary of a dwelling. He was sitting back casually rolling a cigarette, licking the edges of the tissue paper and then stomping the ends as I greeted him placing my brief case on the floor. "Not bloody fair" he said, "Shouldn't be in here" He lit up and inhaled, desperate to convince me he was another innocent man. The cops had stitched him up. He said.

I had pen and paper ready and spread the prosecution statements across the desk. "Got any tabs?" he ventured. Always an urgent request, and, "Can ye` ask wor lass to pay is a visit? Ask hor ta bring some bakki and batteries for me radio."

Occasionally, I took on the mantle of Priest and guiding light, explaining in the simplest terms, how his life was wasting away while in prison while the lives of his wife and children continued without him. I tried to explain that locked in cell for months, even years and unable to enjoy the freedom of the innocent man was foolish. "You are always going to be caught, you know that, so why do you do it?"

Too often, my words fell on deaf or disinterested ears. Only rarely did I detect a dull light glowing behind troubled eye`s as the reality of his predicament sank in weeping and a promise to "go straight." next time.

I listened sympathetically to tales of deprivation, neglect and physical abuse as a child, offering my limited empathy and trying to lift their spirits, but ending conference with my usual sense of humour: "now, don't go away."

*

My staple daily work routine was attending police stations, prepare Briefs for counsel and occasionally to take statements from witnesses to RTA`s: pretty much what I had been doing as a copper. One matter which struck me as odd was that, at the end of a criminal trial one side, be it prosecution or defence had to be lying, yet no one was charged with perjury? I visualised a line of lying witnesses, mostly defence, awaiting sentence.

Having completed a brief for the instructed barrister and wrapped it up in pretty- silk ribbon, I marched along to Counsels` Chambers and arranging a conference, usually in the evening when the courts had closed.

Eric engaged New Court Chambers' and the many competent barristers who would fight the cause, cross examine prosecution witnesses and defend the indefensible... as long as their cash tills rang loudly.

During conferences, I took the opportunity to improve my own legal education, listening intently as counsel produced a bag of legal tricks with the skill of the magician, searching legal precedents and loopholes hidden away in dusty law books hidden away on back shelves. I often looked on with dismay as the evidence of honest witnesses was cut to pieces with the ruthless cunning of a sharp-tongued barrister and it did not take me long to realise that winning or losing depended not on a paradox; the mystery we lawyers call 'justice' but the performance of the best Shakespearian actor.

Then, of course, there is the jury. Some members do not have the intellect of a gnat, barely able to read the oath without careful prompting while others are so biased they have already settled their intention to convict, or acquit, before hearing one word of evidence. Tattoos, dirty fingernail's and demeanour of the witness cementing their decision of guilt or innocence.

One lengthy trial ended in uproar. The Foreman announcing the jury's verdict: "We, the jury, find the defendant not quite guilty of the first charge...and not quite, not guilty of the second charge."

The Judge threw down his pen and scowled in disbelief...but his hands tied.

I longed to be in the legal arena. To taste the cut- and- thrust of cross-examination, to test my legal skills against my opponent and to see the contest played out to its just, or unjust, conclusion. I spent hours hiding away in my room, crouched over my desk, deep in law journals, dissecting the prosecution evidence, probing every sentence in search of that inherent weakness I knew from experience, existed in the prosecution files, my expertise as a former detective and a valued member of the Northumbria Crime Squad serving me well.

The day for admission as a solicitor was drawing near. I would be free to run amok in the Magistrates` Court, to pit my wits against the police (my ex colleagues) and the Crown Prosecution. During a conference with my client at Kenton Bar Crown Court, he showed complete disinterest or ignorance. A thirty years old who had never worked a day in his life and with a long history of offending. My barrister, Michael Hodson, gave him firm advice but his attention was anywhere but on the urgent matter of his pending trial. Michael, an eminent and senior lawyer from New Court Chambers would call him a casualty of character, devoid of the basic skills of intellect and common sense. No matter how much he tried, and he certainly tried to sway him to plead guilty, he only wanted to know one thing: "Am a ganin t` jail?"

Counsel reluctantly accepted defeat and, from the top of his head, he picked a sentence, "If you plead guilty I think you will get six month`s suspended for twelve months" and the conference ended.

I watched him drifting detached, along the corridor and I took myself into the solicitor`s room to wait our call to go into court. and the trial to begin but an hour had lapsed so I decided to find him and try once more. His timely guilty plea would save a great deal of time, the judges always proffer to save court expense.

My search was unsuccessful. I scoured the waiting rooms, the toilets, the small café but he had disappeared. I panicked. Where has he gone? His case called into court, the judge demanding an explanation for his absence, threatening a warrant for his arrest but after much grovelling Michael persuaded the Judge to grant a short adjournment.

"I will stand the case down" the judge glowered passed my barrister at me: "Find him." I didn`t need to be told twice. I was outside the court like a bullet from a gun, racing along the corridor and enquired of a group of yobs who pointed me to the Kenton Bar Pub some four hundred metres north. I found him caressing a pint of beer and an expression of joyful satisfaction, froth dripping off thick lips. "Can I buy you a pint?" he shouted me over to him.

"What the hell are you doing here?" I barked: "The judge is waiting for you."

"I was just telling my mates here. I was lucky. I got six month suspended prison sentence. So I'm celebrating," he raised his glass in salute and I felt like pouring it over his head.

It took me less than thirty seconds to convince him the judge was waiting.

*

I was to appear before a Judge in his private Chambers at Moothall Crown Court. I was to make plea for my client's release on bail from prison, although he had a long history of violence including threats to kill and torture. The defendant would be in prison during the application and I was pleased. I knew he had little chance of success and he may have kicked off with his usual abuse.

The Crown Prosecution Service would raise strong object, demanding he stay in custody and as the time approached we were marched into the Judge's room ready to do battle but, as I stepped through the door His Honour promptly announced: "Mr Gibson, is this application on your client's instructions?" I bowed and conceded the point. The judge had already made up his mind. I was still moving through the door when he said: "Well fought" he grinned at me, "but your client's application is refused"

I did not get a chance utter one word and I turned to walk out as the Judge shouted: "Tell your client the Judge was a bastard and then he will not blame you," he smiled.

Back in the office there was an awkward atmosphere. Something was wrong. Eric had been diagnosed with M.S and sometimes he struggled to attend courts, but Mr Beecham and Mr Peacock were apparently unsympathetic. Profits ruled the practice and Eric was becoming a liability.

11th May 1981 I was admitted to the Roll as a Solicitor and a life changing experience as I assisted Eric in court, an experience much removed from my erstwhile days pulling on a policeman's uniform and fastening the silver buttons. I was now in the big arena, where the intellectuals played hard- ball.

My sudden appearance before the Bench no more than a minor distraction to most lawyers who greeted me well and willing to offer this new boy help and advice. But one solicitor, who's name I shall not mention, treated me like a leaper, keeping me at a distance and believing I was still a cop undercover, seeking to infiltrate the Holy legal sanctum to discover home truths. "You are the last line of defence," he told me sarcastically, as if I was a spy, and I presume he meant I would inform the police what life was really like in the lawyer's underworld where solicitor and clients made pacts Maybe he had something to hide? It took many years to convince him I would fight for my clients with a straight bat, honourably and I never bend the rules.

*

I had been qualified only six months. Eric wanted to talk in confidence. We met up over coffee. "I intend to leave the practice." He was saddened. He said he was not receiving the support he expected then made me a proposition.

"We would open our own office and go into partnership." To my surprise he already sourced offices in the Bigg Market, Newcastle, the first floor above the Half Moon Pub where there were four good size rooms running off a narrow corridor and with lots of passing trade.

His terms were generous offering me 49% of the shares. An ex- copper recently qualified and offered a full partnership. A handshake settled the matter and I took a giant leap forward.

"I've spoken to Clive Hindle," Eric said. "Clive has offices at North Shields. He has the lease on the Bigg Market offices and has agreed to sublease them to us." Things were moving fast.

I discussed the move with Anne. She worried. She was right to worry. I had to ask myself if I was getting in too deep too soon, but we decided to go for it. In for a penny in for a pound and, with much trepidation, I resigned my position and moved my few personal belongings into the new offices then waited for Eric to join me.

Anne organised the rooms ordering a telephone, typewriter and stationery. I set off into the court in search of clientele. I needed legal aide to keep me going. Until Eric joined me I was breaking the Law Society rules: For the first three year's a newly qualified solicitor must be supervised by an experienced solicitor. I needed Eric urgently.

Anne helped to paint the doors, walls and tidy the rooms. I grabbed an armful of empty files, dropping them into my new brief case and headed to the court in the vein hope that I would pick up a client and much needed cash. Someone had to pay the rent and service charges. We could only hold out for a few weeks.

Anne sat near the silent phone, her pen in hand, waiting.

I struck lucky and represented a man charged with being drunk and disorderly then another caught urinating in the street, not a bad start. In a few weeks I was up and running, scratching around the court corridors picking up petty shop- lifters, domestic assaults and a teenager who had stolen a pedal cycle.

In the afternoons, I twiddled my thumbs waiting for Eric to join me then I took a call from Eric: "Sorry Bert, but I am too ill. I am going to retire to concentrate on my health" Our partnership was over before it began. Eric was ill, I understood that, but he had left me in a very precarious situation. That phone call had ended my legal career. Without supervision, I would have to close the office. I could not earn a living.

I was frantic. Anne worried. I never envisaged this happening. I had a mortgage, a wife and two children to support.

Clive Hindle, solicitor, was my lifeline and I will always be grateful to him. He offered to employ me as his assistant. He said I would remain in the Bigg Market on the understanding that all profits from my work we shared 50-50.

"You will be liable for the overheads," he said, "the gas, electricity, the works." I had no choice. I had to accept or return to the police force, begging for my job.

There was no time for anger or upset. I had to find clients and quickly. I had to build the practice from scratch and I searched everywhere for work.

Help arrived in the form of my ex colleagues who channelled burglars and thieves and public order offenders my way, helping build a practice and pay my debts. I owe them a great deal.

Clive saw the work gushing though the door and profits soaring. He wanted more, insisting I must sign a 45 pages partnership deed. I took it home and read it, carefully. Clive had control of everything, including me. It appointed him Chief Executive with unquestioned authority, leaving me unable even to buy toilet rolls without his approval. I had to consult him on every decision. I could not hire staff, buy furniture or make any decisions of importance, but had to work day and night without assistance.

I needed advice. I approached Mr Meikle solicitor and respected member of my profession, the senior partner of Keenleyside and Forster, Collingwood Street, Newcastle.

"An excellent partnership deed" he told me, "A work of art...but for goodness sake don't sign it," he insisted, "It`s all one sided, and most certainly not in your interest."

I could not be Clive`s partner. Not on those terms and broke the news to him. He was annoyed and his response was to demand I get out of his offices but then he made me an offer. He would sell me the lease for £5000, knowing I could not possibly raise that amount.

Anne and I were struggling financially. We had no spare cash. We had been living on egg and chips but somehow I had to find the money. I had never thought in my wildest dreams that joining the legal profession could cause so much stress. I felt trapped, but I needed to be strong and to stand on my own two feet. I could see Anne worrying. I worried for us both. "Where was our next penny come from?" Welcome to the legal profession.

I made an appointment to see my bank manager begging for a loan. He was a tower of strength, supporting and encouraging me and offering the funds I needed. It was a beginning and I arranged for a private investigator to drop the cheque into Clive's office and to come back with a receipt.

The name: Bert Gibson & Co. hung proudly over the door, but very little in the way of furniture or carpets behind it.

I made an executive decision. I appointed Anne my secretary, receptionist, tea- maker, sharpener of pencils, cleaner and general goffer. The Bigg Market office was my new home but it would be some time before I could afford the luxury of carpets on the floor or a working typewriter.

At 3:00pm school days, Anne would leave to collect our children. I stayed behind doodling on scrap paper and planning our empire, forecasting where I hoped to be in 5 years whilst willing the telephone to ring.

Before going off to the court in the morning I would stand on parade before Anne, her majesty, as she gave me the once over, checking my tie was straight, shoes polished and trouser zip up. "You may have empty pockets but you are not stepping out of that door looking untidy." She insisted. Having passed muster I strolled up the Bigg Market to the Magistrates' Court, full more of hope than realistic expectation in search for clientele. The afternoons I waited patiently for footsteps: someone to walk through the door. It was desperate times, but I was not for giving up.

Weeks scraping by became months, my one filing cabinet filling up and a light began to shine at the end of a long dark tunnel. Cases of simple theft, assaults and burglary rolled through my door and my name occasionally appeared in the local press. I checked my piggy bank. It rattled. I looked for a typist and junior to ease Anne's work. She looked after the accounts and wages.

Life was a gamble, a game of chance. Move in one direction and succeed, turn in another and fail. Where the dice falls, we never know, but we learn to deal with the hand given,

Then that incomprehensible thing called luck. To be in the right place at the right time when an opportunity arose, and grasp it with both hands. This was my initiation into the legal profession.

As a Police Officer, I had fought hard to pass the interviews, the medicals. I studied for the promotion exams, passing the Sergeants examination with high marks and the Inspectors promotion exam two years later. I was proud to wear the uniform of Constable and Anne often remarked that I had an obsessive fascination for the law, and Anne should know she often talked at the breakfast table to my head, my eyes buried in law journals.

As a copper, I spent my first two year`s pounding the streets of Blyth. Then to Berwick, Whitley Bay, and Guide Post, driving police motor- cars and riding police bikes, but I was learning about people I transferred into CID, then securing a rare vacancy in the Serious Incident Squad, Market Street, a specialist Crime Unit and one of only four detectives trained to deal with murders robberies and complex/protracted crimes.

Summer 1973, I was heading along the corridor on the fourth floor of Market Street Police Station when I overheard a Chief Inspector discussing his days at university. He drew me to one side and asked if I would like to apply for a law degree. "Three years of hard study, Bert," I had no idea what that entailed or if I would be successful, but he had faith in me and I sent off a report, in triplicate, to HQ.

"Never pass up an opportunity," my father would say. University was for clever buggers, high achievers and now, in my early-thirties, I found myself sitting amongst the highbrows half my age and studying law.

I put my head down and worked, first shown how to find High Court Judgements hidden away in thick volumes of 18th and 19th century books: the English Legal System, Contract and the law of Torts with a splash of psychology thrown in as an optional extra. The second year I shared my limited time with two active children, exams followed year on year and somehow, despite many interruptions, I stumbled and fumbled my way to the end with an Honours Degree.

An interview with the Deputy Chief Constable followed with a firm promise of "the next promotion" but found myself working at Wallsend and then Forest Hall Police Stations and being passed- over in favour of other officers with less experience. I queried their decision: "You have been away from the job for three years. You have to prove yourself all over again." I was too ambitious to tread water for three years and with no firm prospects of promotion, despite a promise I began to look elsewhere.

*

A murder broke in the City Centre. A man found dead in the street. I was sent in to help investigate expecting to work in the Incident Room, the hub of the investigation, my former experience being of value, but instead delegated door- to- door enquiries, foot- slogging. My future lay elsewhere. I heard whispers of a vacancy for an Articled Clerk (trainee Solicitor) and, tongue in cheek, applied. My interview was successful and my career began to move in another direction. I had sleepless nights wondering if I could pass the solicitor`s finals and then what kind of contribution this ex copper would make as a solicitor. To some extent, I had the inside track. I knew the law in practice. I knew when and how my former police colleagues pasted over cracks in the evidence and cut corners to gain a conviction: where truth and fiction often merged.

"I will put in a good word with the judge," some would promise but not kept. Catching and charging the criminal was often like a game of chess, keeping some juicy bits of evidence close to our chest, waiting for the suspect to trip himself up then seizing the moment. Sadly, I have to say, some officers were prepared to strengthen a weak case, but I will say no more about that, justifying their actions with the excuse: "he needed to be taken off our streets."

*

The Magistrates' Court became my home. I was building my reputation as a straight bat, representing the mildly dishonest, the downright evil and the innocent few caught up in an unintended circumstance. I was learning facets of my new arena and its many participants.

I recall in the 1960's as a young copper, having to attended the Assize and the Quarter Sessions. (Yes, I am that old). Those ancient courts replaced in 1972 with the Crown Courts and Judges' appointed to that High Office by Her Majesty the Queen.

In the 19th century, Magistrates' sat individually to hear criminal cases but, after 1849, two or more Magistrate's sat together in what we then called the Petty Sessional Area. A Stipendiary Magistrate, usually solicitor, with seven years calling or a barrister, sitting alone to hear criminal or civil cases but from August 2000, The District Judge replaced the Stipendiary and I was delighted to see my good friend and colleague, Stephen Earl appointed District Judge.

Judge Earl now sits in the Newcastle Magistrates' Court dispensing wisdom and fairness, and receiving well-deserved respect from his former colleagues.

Chapter Three

I ventured into the detention cells below the Newcastle Magistrates' Court. It would be my first experience of representing a prisoner and I was on tenterhooks not knowing what to expect, how he would react. Did he know me as a copper? Down the stone steps and along the corridor, a journey I had made so many times before to put prisoners inside. Now my roll was reversed.

He had been charged with robbery, an offence only heard before a Judge at the Crown Court. My roll would be to help get him there, hopefully on bail but the offence carried a life sentence. PC Andy Ashwell led me along the corridor and unlocked the cell door. He winked as I stepped inside and introduced myself. A well build man, he was sitting on the edge of the wooden bench, his knees tucked under his chin. He jumped to his feet, jaw set and angry shouting abuse at me as if I was the one who had put him there. I had expected anger, anxiety, unrest but he was demanding his right to bail and we both knew his chances were slim to nil.

Prisoners with a long list of convictions always knew their rights and this man had an armful. If I had been a copper, I would have looked him straight in the eye and told him about the real world. He would get what he deserved, a long stretch in prison, then I would lock the door and go off to celebrate. As his lawyer, I had to do my best to console him. To understand why he had ended up, again, in this dreadful mess and a long prison sentence looming.

I fumbled for my note pad. "I want bail," he shouted. I decided not to tell him the odds against that. I scribbled down a few pointers: address, bail conditions, surrender passport and stay away from witnesses, In a few short minutes, I would climb the stairs and make my way into court knowing I would fail. Not a happy thought, but I encouraged him to remember he could appeal today's decision to the Judge at the crown court if I failed...

Petrol used in fire death house–claim

A FIREMAN smelt meths or petrol at the scene of a fatal house blaze, Newcastle Crown Court was told today.

A Pakistani businessman died after an arson attack on a home in Heaton he shared with his two brothers and their families.

After the fire was extinguished, an officer noted a strong smell of methylated spirits or petrol in the area around the front door.

Mohammed Zafir was badly burned in the fire and died almost a month later.

Mr. Iqbal and his brother, Mohammed Naji and Mushtaq Ahmed ran a number of clothing shops in Newcastle and around the North-East.

Two 16-year-olds, Peter Drape, of Weldon Crescent and Mark Vasey, of Kelvin Grove, both of Heaton, Newcastle, deny murdering Mr. Iqbal and arson at Cheltenham Terrace, Heaton.

Mr. James Chadwin, Q.C., prosecuting, said the two youths poured inflammable liquid through the letter box of the house and then ignited it.

Having previously heard some noise Mr. Iqbal was kneeling behind the door when the attack occurred and was severely burned.

The jury were told it was believed Mr. Iqbal died "almost by mistake," as the attack was really against his brother Mohammed Naji, who was in London, on holiday with his wife and five children.

Station officer, Keith Alexander Stewart, of Tyne Wear Fire Brigade, said when his tender arrived at the house, a man was hanging over the ledge of a small front bedroom. The window was broken.

When he went into the room to the window the room was hot and smokey. Other firemen arrived and they carried the man, Mr. Iqbal, out.

He said the fir in the entrance hall had been severe, and concentrated in the area around the front door. There was a great deal of damage and heat build-up around the door.

"I picked up a piece of carpet and there was a smell of meths and petrol, some sort of inflammable material."

The fire started on the carpet immediately behind the front door.

Mr. Iqbal suffered burns to his head, neck and arms, hands and shoulders.

PROCEEDING

just to keep him calm. I did not want him turning his anger on me. I had seen many instances of abuse towards solicitors and reputations going down the pan.

I scribbled down a few words of denial, always something to tag onto my speech. "It wasn't me" he protested, "the copper's stitched me up." I had heard that so many times but, in this case, the prosecution evidence was bomb proof, and if I as his solicitor, did not think he deserved bail, why would the Magistrates?

I flicked through the prosecution page's, five statements pointed to the defendant. I read the summary loud. He listened.

He had waited in the shadows for the Rent Collector to walk passed. He knew his routine and that he carried large amounts of cash. As his victim wandered passed, he struck him a heavy blow to the head with an iron bar, grabbing the bag and running off, leaving him lying in a pool of blood. A partial description led the police to his home and the stolen cash recovered. I hoped the weight of the evidence would sink in. Make him understand he would receive a sentence measured in years not months. I slammed the cell door closed, more out of habit, and left him shouting abuse at Andy, demanding his cigarettes, "I know my rights."

I took a seat on the front bench in the remand court, my nerves jangling and beads of sweat peppering my brow. The public gallery was full. like- minded hooligans, society's drop- outs and misfits having a free show, those fortunate not to be occupying another cell. Friends looking on, gloating, as friend's faced the degradation ceremony of being sent to prison. They looked excited wanting the show to begin and to know for how long. Today was like a holiday, a day out for those in the gallery; a place to go for entertainment

I read my scribbled notes. I would offer the court a condition of residence and reporting daily to the police station. I would offer a curfew to keep him off the streets at night. I marked the prospects of success at 2 out of 100.

The court clerk wandered in, piles of paper under her arm and occupied her position in front of the three empty seats soon to be filled by the Bench. I let my eyes search the legal arena. A place where the solicitor`s reputation is won or lost in a fifteen minute hearing. With this client I didn`t think I could stay on my feet that long.

The Neanderthals' in the public gallery, demanded success and nothing less, most of them back street lawyers, expecting solicitor`s to end up on the floor fighting.

Basil Mellon, a lawyer of immense experience and a formidable reputation, was quietly reading a newspaper and looking decidedly bored. How I envied him. His laid- back attitude. For him, it was another day at the office.

He threw a glance to this new boy. Maybe he saw my hand shaking. "Put your legal aid forms in son…" he said, "then you know you`re going to get paid." A weight lifted from my shoulders but only for a moment. He had given me perspective and told me the importance of the proceedings: money first client second

P.C. Andy Ashwell brought my client into the dock. He had a record of escaping and handcuffed. That was not going to help my cause. They stood facing the Magistrates. Andy winked at me. It was a knowing wink formed from many years of experience in the cells. He knew my prisoner, his reputation, his habits, and soon he knew he would be tripping back down the stairs enjoying a free ride to Durham Prison.

The prosecution opened the case eloquently, demanding the prisoner be remand into custody, "This was a violent robbery" he said, "He is a danger to society," I swallowed hard, the Court listened to every word and, foolishly, I agreed. Now it was my turn. I searched my notes, something for inspiration. What would I say? How would I begin? My knees trembling I rose slowly to my feet and my mouth began to move, how I do not know, my voice somewhere resonating high in the ornate ceiling, my mouth dry as sticks. I think I spoke for three minutes then dropped onto my seat with a face the colour of a beetroot.

The Magistrates did me the honour of retiring to consider the issues, but their verdict was inevitable. Andy gave a hushed "tut" mouthing: "he's going to prison," almost in a song.

The Bench returned to confirm my expectations and the prisoner began to shout, thankfully not at me, then he was off to Durham prison, with loud curses and expletives echoing down the stairs.

I had made my first appearance in the court… and had lost but it was over. Now I was an experienced advocate… with a throbbing head.

*

6th August 1981 and two boys, 15 years of age arrested for murder. "Do you want to represent one of them, Bert?" The Detective Superintendent asked and I shot over Byker Bridge to the Police Station recalling my experiences investigating such murders and hoping it would prove valuable to the boy I would represent.

Murder cases were not new to me. I had experienced investigations of this kind, from start to finish, collating evidence, proving every step towards a conviction. The murder of Lieutenant-colonel John Stevenson ran through my mind. The Commandant at the Army Training Camp at Otterburn, Northumberland had answered a knock at his front door. It was late and when the door opened, he was shot dead, IRA style. The gunman also shot two Police Officers at the Percy Arms Hotel, thankfully not seriously, as they tried to arrest him.

Sean O'Connell, Raymond Kane and Barry Reed were convicted of murder and sentenced to life in prison, O'Connell receiving a further fifteen years for the attempted murder of the two detectives.

The Custody Sergeant led me through to the detention block where I introduced myself to the tall slim boy curled up in the corner. A police officer sitting outside the open cell door told me, "his mother is on her way." The officer had been delegated, suicide watch, keeping the boy under constant observation. A social worker had already spoken to the boy. He would act in loco parentis (guardian) until his mother arrived for the formal interview. I sat next to him, dropping my briefcase on the floor, passing a few gentle words of encouragement, getting him on my side and promising: "I am here to help."

"Have the police questioned you?" I needed to know: "Have you made admissions?" The boy was no stranger to police stations. He had been chalking up a list of minor misdemeanours for a year or two, but this was big league: life changing. He would not be playing on his bike for a while. I needed to know if he had said something to harm his defence. He shook his head his moist eyes confused, anxious. He was trying to be strong and brave, his young face an expression of false denial but he was terrified.

"I didn't do it," he pleaded, wiping his nose. I nodded. I needed him to know I would accept anything he wanted to tell me. I had to gain his confidence. In gasps of distress, he denied the murder. "I don't know why they arrested me."

I needed to know if he had an alibi: where he had been that day. I needed to know his movements, minute by minute, to get inside of his head and to see through his young eyes. Play it back like a video, every second of his movements that day.

Alan Findlay, a former police officer and now an experienced solicitor, would represent the other boy. He and I met in the early 1960`s at Blyth Division when we worked together. Then we were new recruits, probationers, fresh out of the training college. I followed Alan to Berwick-on Tweed where he worked as a detective before he qualified as a solicitor. Now a partner with solicitor`s Mincoff, Science and Gold, his experience would be of mutual benefit to our clients.

My client`s mother arrived, stressed and upset but calm enough to discuss with me her sons habits, hobbies, friends and what time he had left the house that day. I needed her on my side. The prospect of an acquittal for a charge of murder was very slim, almost impossible, but I could not tell her son that or her.

Alan and I got our heads together. We needed to sing from the same hymn sheet, to know if the boys had been together throughout. Was one boy responsible, but blaming the other? I had to keep all options open. We prepared a plan of action.

There was no conflict between the boys, no variance in their instructions or their movements for that day. We would prepare the defence and discuss progress but always fight our individual corners: a fight of uneven proportions. My legal team, consisting of me, against the investigative might of the entire Northumbria Police Force and with forensic agents and experts on tap and no expense spared.

The Police had a head start. We would not be working on an even playing field. Their investigations had been running for several hours ending with the arrest of the boys. Their evidence collated and paginated into reams of paper, photos and forensic reports. My work was to begin.

I instructed Mary McMurray QC, to lead and Bill Hannah, Barrister and a retired Police Chief Superintendent who had mountains of experience. Mary had a laser sharp mind and the ability to dissect evidence with the skill of a surgeon, able to uncover half-truths, imperfections and improbabilities in the evidence and search for the weakest link to slice open.

Bill Hannah, a man of immense practical experience could look at a man, or a boy, in the eye and get at the truth, weigh his character. He would be invaluable to our defence: a master psychologist and an excellent lawyer. I had found the best legal team in the North of England.

The facts disclosed. A house in Cheltenham Terrace, Heaton, had been petrol bombed and the occupant, Mohammed Iqbal a married man, burned to death. The police were convinced the two boys were responsible. They said the youngsters had sneaked up to the front door, armed with a petrol can and poured the contents through the letterbox, then lit it.

Mr. Iqbal lived with his family in the first floor flat. He heard a noise and went to investigate, descending the stairs to the front door. He bent over to peer through the letterbox when there was an explosion as the petrol ignited and, in the confined space, he had no chance as the flames shot high engulfing him instantly.. He died a terrible, painful, death.

I visited the flat. A typical Victorian Terrace split in to two homes and private front doors. A narrow unkempt lawn, only a few yards wide, extended to the rampant hedge and public footpath.

The inner hall was black and chard, the flames having travelled up the stairs and into the lounge.

The Police were adamant the two boys had meant to target the deceased's brother, Mohammed Naji, who fortunately, was in London.

We represented the boys at Newcastle Youth Court. There was more press than public at the hearing. I told the court my young client was no angel. He would deny the murder. I asked for bail, but remanded.

Back in my office I found myself fighting off probing questions from the local press, anxious to get the inside story: "Did they do it? Why has this happened? Would they be pleading guilty?" I ushered them out.

The boys remained in custody for several months while my team sifted through the prosecution case, cross- referencing statement's, ready to challenge those seeking to give evidence of opinion and hearsay, rather than hard facts. My client's father could take the pressure no longer and committed suicide. The boy was devastated and wanted to attend the funeral: another problem.

The trial began at the Moothall Crown Court. We were ready for the fight. Mary and Bill were prepared. No holds barred. The evidence swung one way and then the other, Mary cutting deep wounds in the prosecution case. There was no evidence of petroleum on our client or his clothing, no forensic evidence to put them at the scene. One civilian witness who lived across the street said he saw two boys carrying a can. We challenged his evidence showing with photos, the rampant overgrown hedge at the front door obstructing his view.

The jury retired, deliberating for several hours, then returned with a verdict of Not Guilty. The boys were innocent but they had spent nearly a year in jail.

The verdict told the world they were innocent, but my client would return home without a father, a lifetime conviction in its self.

I had won my first murder trial, but there was nothing to celebrate.

My client`s family and the Iqbal family had both lost their father. Tragedy had struck two innocent families. Their lives would never be the same again.

*

My next appointment was late and my thoughts drifted to my friend and former colleague, Chief Inspector Colin Paver now sadly dead.

Colin and I met at the Detective Training College, Wakefield and having left the police force we kept in touch. I watched with interest his progression through the ranks, his last post as Commander at Hexham Police Station. We often met for lunch, chatting about days gone by, some happy some sad. One incident at Ashington Police Station came to the fore when he and I arrested a man suspected of sexually abusing children. We wanted him off the streets. The public wanted a quick arrest. There was an outcry, but the suspect was no stranger to our cells and knew his rights. He refused to speak or admit his guilt. He knew we only had the word of children and they would be terrified to attend court. "Who would believe them", he would say arrogantly.

We spent hours questioning him and then putting him back into his cell, slamming the door, but he knew his silence could see him walk free. We had to find a way to deal with him.

By 11p.m, we had gotten nowhere. We had been on duty from early morning and wanted to go home to our families. We adjourned to the canteen and, over a mug of coffee, we decided our prisoner`s future. The Magistrates` Court sat immediately behind the police station but under the same roof, with the entrance to both building`s adjoining It was midnight when we decided to hold our own special court.

Colin with his posh southern accent would sit as Chairman. I went into the Duty Inspector`s room and borrowed his, cap and his police tunic with all its silver buttons and pips on the shoulders. I decided I would prosecute, pulling the peek cap forward over my eyes and taking up a position in front of the dock where the prisoner would stand.

Colin looked imposing there on the Bench and the court lights lowered. Two uniformed officers on meal break escort the prisoner from the cell, along the linking corridor and into the Dock. I began, the prisoner shouting his innocence and demanding his lawyer. Colin ordered him to silence. I disguised my voice, speaking as eloquently as I could, opening the facts. Colin listened, studiously, giving an occasional `tut` at appropriate moments.

I relayed the facts, a little embellished and a sprinkle of fiction thrown in to the pot while the prisoner gasped his denial. Colin ignored him bringing the gavel down hard and demanding silence in his court, pretending to scribble down a few notes, playing the part masterfully.

The defendant was visibly shocked then Colin announced, "Three years in jail. Take him back to his cell," The prisoner crying out for justice, his protestations echoing along the corridor to his cell.

We dressed and left him stewing for an hour, then casually told him he was on his way to Durham Prison where men like him, "would face violent men who ate perverts for breakfast." We ignored his pleas for justice suggesting when he arrives at the prison he seek the Governor`s protection. "Ask for segregation." We closed the cell door, turning the heavy key.

In silence, we waited listening to him prowl the room mumbling anxiously words of abuse. We let the time pass then made him a proposition. In return for an admission of guilt, we would cancel the court and start again. We promised him credit for his guilty plea and a discount on his sentence, suggesting he may not go to jail. With two fingers crossed. "We could put in a good word for you."

He nodded and we were all over him like a long lost brother, patting him on the back, providing cigarettes and a large mug of hot coffee. He gave information about the abuse that only a guilty man would know and not disclosed to the public. We were satisfied he was responsible.

The next morning, and ignorant of the previous night events, the Duty Inspector prosecuted, submitting the defendant`s voluntary admissions to the court. We hid in the wings as the properly constituted court gave him six months in prison. We were happy. He was happy, but more important the children of Ashington would be safe.

During one of our lunch`s Colin mentioned the Clerk to Hexham Magistrates` was moving on to pasture new and a social event organised in the Great Room of Hexham Old Castle. He invited me to go along where probation, magistrate`s and local dignitaries would be in attendance to wish the Clerk success.

In the Great Room, we all assembled in an arc around the Clerk, listening to speeches, some hilarious, some tearfully embarrassing then a young member of the court staff moved through the crowd to present him with a gift, beautifully wrapped, the size of a shoe-box. He looked overawed, flushed with emotion then another member of staff rushed forward, grabbing the gift out of his hands and throwing it violently to the ground, jumping, stamping and kicking it around the floor with the sound of glass shattering into a million pieces.

There were gasps of astonishment. Sound of muffled confusion from the audience, then a more senior member of staff stepped forward to present his real gift, and we saw the joke.

Another surprise awaited him, lurking in the shadows in the form was a shapely buxom young woman, skimpily dressed, whip in hand. She tip toed from the darkness, creeping up behind our celebrity, her whip held high then grabbed him in places indecent, dragging him backwards across the desk, his face flushed and pretending to whip his buttocks, calling out: "You have been a very naughty Mr Court Clerk."

Some dignitaries didn`t know whether to laugh or to leave. Colin and I were having great fun and my solicitor colleague, Peter MacDonald, shouted out earnestly: "Oh, I have been much naughtier than him," bending over and pleading with her to spank him.

The evening was a great success with much laughter and many drinks into the late hours.

Chapter Four

My brother, Eddie, worked as a Detective at Byker. He invited me to watch a game of football. A league match played by men over forty years of age with birth certificates, driving licences and even passports produced as confirmation of age. "We might be coppers, but they trust no one," he said. Apparently, there had been allegations of driving licences `doctored` and passports forged to enable the underage to play.

It was a bright Saturday morning in September 1983. Northumbria Police Over-Forties would play against Del a Rue, a tough match with former semi-professional`s in their side.

Eddie and I wandered into the changing room where I met former colleagues, listening to them chatting excitedly about recent arrests, promotions in the ranks and the match as they slipped on royal blue shirts and pulled on their boots. Initially greeted with cries of Judas for daring to leave the force and join the enemy, followed with jovial banter. Tom Brown, the manager and an ex Middlesbrough professional gave the pep talk before they went onto the field, reminding the team of the strength of their opponents.

"Got your boots?" Tom asked my brother but looking at me. "We are two players short."

There had been an incident in City Centre the night before requiring several officers to work overtime.

A football shirt thrown our way and quickly drafted into the side. My protestations of being under age, ignored: "That`s okay", Tom said, "we can have one ringer" he winked, "They will never notice. Your silver hair and a face full of wrinkles will hide the truth. He got a laugh from the team. "Anyway you`re are an ex- copper so you`re eligible."

I loved football and Tom did not need ask me twice I threw on a pair of borrowed boots and the game began in earnest with Del a Rue bombarding our goal like a swarm of angry wasps, but by half time, and from pure luck, we were one goal ahead Our centre forward,. Dave Billham slipping the ball passed their goalkeeper. The match ended 4-1 to us and I became a fixture playing every game on the left wing.

Thereafter on a Saturday morning, we met outside of Gateshead Police Station for away games, travelling through to Sunderland, Durham or South Shields in the police van. One copper, who shall remain nameless, openly discussed a certain woman police officer, referring to her as "Kipper Knickers." Puzzled by this remark; I asked him why?"

"You would understand if you were with her in a panda car for eight hours on a hot sunny day and the windows shut." He held his nose in the air, "Fwarr, BO."

I introduce two of my solicitor colleagues to the team, Geoffrey Forester, who had an office in South Shields and Norman Peacock, my former boss at Alan Henderson Beecham and Lee, both making valuable contributions as we climbed the league and eventually through to a number of cup finals.

*

Learning the art of advocacy and watching my contemporaries at work, I noticed certain phrases popping out from the mouths of the more eloquently verbose lawyers, and decided to adopt them for myself.

Some, you will have heard, either on television or during fictional trial's such as Judge Deed or Rumbold of the Bailey: "If you are with me, My Lord," or "The acid test"…and.. "The thread running through… " are regularly verbalised and often to the advantage of the defendant. It also struck me that barristers hogged the lime light, always in search of publicity… for example on television and in films, barristers refer to each other as 'my Learned Friend' when, in truth, they are no more learned than we solicitors. In fact, barristers have to pass further legal examinations to qualify as solicitor, whereas we solicitors need only don wig and gown and take pupillage.

When I appeared in the Magistrates' I would occasionally use the phrases, mixing them with what we lawyers call verbal garbage, something to pad out a failing application or mitigation. Enough for the defendant to believe we had tried hard. But, let`s be honest, how many defendants would understand what we solicitors say? Some Magistrates' do not understand, but those phrases frequently made the difference between a good speech, and liberty, and a prison sentence for the defendant.

Sometime, to allay the boredom of advocacy, we amused ourselves with silly word games. Whilst rising to our feet to address the Bench, a random word whispered in his ear, which he must somehow introduce into his speech. It takes quite a bit of verbal dexterity and grammatical manipulation to include words such as, Squaw (a female Red Indian) or pussy-willow, into the speech of someone charged with urinating in the street.

*

As the years rolled on, I watched with dismay and concern at the seedier, darker, side of my profession. Lawyers, who I am not prepared to name, prepared to bend rules and take liberties with the truth and regularly flaunted the rules in favour of his client.

I have heard lawyers whispering legal defences to clients to beat a conviction, when a timely guilty plea would be in the client`s best interest. Cases listed for trial with frivolous, unrealistic, expectations of an acquittal, sometimes in the hope the victim: a battered a wife, a timid witness, may be too frightened to attend court to give evidence. Not guilty pleas tendered days before Christmas for the sole purpose of allowing the client to spend the festive season with his family, knowing his next stop was prison.

I was appalled at some underhand tricks to gain the defendant`s favour and often in the hope of enticing him to stay with the firm: offering money or a free ride for the family of his client to visit the defendant in prison. Vouchers and postal orders exchanged for goods in prison, gifts as an inducement to keep the defendant and his family on their books. All in the interest of profits

Was this defeating the legal process? Was it in the best interest of the client? You decide. I believe the solicitors were bringing discredit and shame to a proud profession.

More worrying is the solicitor prepared to break the rules: deliberately act dishonestly in pursuit of his client. Lawyers inclined to protect the guilty soon come unstuck when the very people they have protected turn and grass on them to the police to save their own skin. Lawyer`s will never learn that our criminal client is OUR WORST ENEMY and must be kept at arm`s length.

Lawyer`s touting for business, attempting to sway defendant`s away from their own solicitor. Solicitor`s standing outside the doors of the court, approaching those about to enter and asking if they had a solicitor, offering a business card and their services when we have a Duty Solicitor Scheme for those unrepresented defendants who are given free legal advice and help to progress his case. The Duty Solicitor is the only one permitted to approach unrepresented defendants and then to ask only two questions. "Do you have your own solicitor? Would you like me to contact a solicitor of your choice?" Sadly, too often that trust is lost when the Duty Solicitor of that day encourages the defendant to abandon his choice and turn to him.

I am saddened to say, solicitors` DO commit criminal offences, although very rarely, but in the mistaken belief, he is helping his client. I have heard of examples of lawyers moving stolen property out of reach of the police, harbouring stolen property in their office and under the pretext of legal privilege. If caught, and they often are, the lawyer is instantly struck of the roll and loses his right to work. In his case, jail is inevitable and good riddance too.

We do not want dishonest people in our profession and, I repeat, the defendant will blame his solicitor at every turn, every opportunity. SO DO

NOT DO IT.

Thankfully, few lawyers are inclined that way but one is too many.

*

A question posed by my university lecturer: "Outline the roll of the solicitor as the political moralist." That question defeated many law students and I confess it was sometime before I fully understood the answer. `Do we lawyers have to conspicuously follow the rule of law? Should we refuse to do so when the law is clearly an ass? Can we put hand on heart and say our legal system protects the honest and convicts only the guilty? In the 19th Century, a High Court Judge remarked.

"The law does not deal in honest errors but the malice of mankind," sadly time has proved him wrong, as many an innocent defendant has been convicted on tainted, false evidence or incompetent lawyers. Do the jury get it right? Are they capable of testing evidence?

An absent-minded, elderly woman and heretofore of impeccable character, may erroneously drop her intended shop purchases into her own handbag bag instead of the trolley provided. It happens. Elderly folk do that sought of thing, but she is arrested, handcuffed and marched through the shop in front of gawping eyes then detained in a police cell for hours. If she survives the trauma of that ordeal, she will face the full weight of our legal system, as if she were a professional criminal and, like it or not, she will have to prove her innocence. The idea that the prosecution must establish proof beyond a reasonable doubt is, in my view, a fiction. A test bandied about by jurists drowning in their own misaligned reality.

It concerns me that lawyers appointed to the high office of Judge have a leaning toward the prosecution and more than a settled mind to a conviction. Thirty years in this profession has not changed my mind. When a police officer relays his evidence to the court, it is rare indeed to cast it to one side as unreliable. I have been a copper. I know what happens Pocket note book`s made up at the time and all that.

To survive in this daily degradation ceremony the solicitor needs his wit and humour. A solicitor in urgent need of the toilet stopped by Court Usher: "your client wants to see you in court three." The solicitor replied, "Tell him to wait. I can only deal with one shit at a time."

A trial fixed and several prosecution witnesses attended to give their evidence, but my client was absent. I handed the Chairman a doctor's sick note, and humbly asked for an adjournment. The Chairman read the medical note and asked me: "This doctor's note says the defendant has a sore shoulder? Why would that prevent him from attending this court?" I replied calmly and pan faced, "Sir, I have a degree in law, not medicine. I don't know."

My adjournment, reluctantly grant, I turned to leave and the Chairman called out to me: "Mr Gibson, if you ever stop being a lawyer… be an actor." I smiled.

A well respected and experienced solicitor was about to make a heart rendering application for his client's bail but first he whispered to me. "I'm going to marry that magistrate," drawing my attention to an elegant lady, smartly dressed, on the left of the Chairman, but when the magistrates' announced their verdict to remand his client into custody he stormed out shouting, "the weddings off."

*

It was 11 30pm on a Friday night. I was to attend Gateshead Police Station to see a client in the cells. George Henderson was the Custody Sergeant. He and I had joined the Police Force way back in 1964, sharing the same dormitory at the Police College and we became good friends

George asked if I would to see my client in the cell: "as the interview rooms are full." leading me along the corridor and unlocking the cell door. I entered to speak to the suspect, plonking myself down beside him. George apologised for having to lock me inside, "for security reasons, Bert," and, "just ring the bell when you are ready to leave." The door slammed shut, the heavy lock engaged I opened my note pad to chat to my client.

My instructions noted and legal advice given, I rang the bell: no response. I pressed again holding my thumb on the button; nothing. My client looked hard at me, a look of suspicion: "Are you a real solicitor or have you been locked up as well?" I played down the obvious embarrassment suggesting the sergeant was a busy man, "he will be here in a moment", then the door unlocked and George stuck his head inside shouting at me: "What the hell do you want? I`ve told you you`re staying in for court in the morning," then slamming the door closed again before I could utter a word. I listened as heavy footsteps echoed and faded along the corridor. I shot a glance at my client. He stared questioningly back at me, moving a few feet to the far end of the bench, an expression of concern.

George was a prankster; he had been a joker at the Police College, but in here, with the door locked, what could I do? I thought his Sergeant`s stripes would have calmed him, then the door flew open and George stepped inside, a broad smile and tendering his profuse apologise. "Why didn`t you let me know you wanted to be out, Bert?" he winked, patting me on the shoulder: "You just had to ring the bell." He pressed it several times to prove it was working.

We exchanged a few choice words along the corridor as he headed for the female block, pausing at an open toilet, inviting me to look in.
 A woman, in her mid-thirties, and clearly comatose was hanging off the edge of the toilet seat; her bra twisted awkwardly across her bare shoulders, exposing her rather large melons. Her head rested awkwardly against the cubicle wall, her knickers crumpled around her ankles showing her dirt-encrusted toes.

George pointed: "Now Bert," he said in a business tone, "I need your legal opinion. Is she fit to be interviewed?"

I cursed him as I walked away.

Chapter Five

It was midnight, late autumn, a call took me to Clifford Street Police Station and what happened could have seen me struck off. The Custody Sergeant escorted me to the detention room where I spread my papers on the desk, my brief case at my feet and waited. The desk and the two chairs screwed to the floor as a precaution, preventing riotous prisoner's picking them up during acts of temper. I squeezed onto the seat, my long legs tucked under the desk.

The defendant, a man in his mid-thirties, detained on suspicion of burgling of Public House where a large quantity of cash, in the form of £10 notes, were stolen from the safe.

I was rummaging through my briefcase when the prisoner entered the room escorted by a burly constable and the handcuffs removed. He sat opposite watched in silence as the officer withdrew, closing the door. A small observation window was in the door at eye level for officers to see inside, but unable to hear our `privileged` conversation.

"I'm innocent Mr Gibson," he whispered to me, leaning across the desk but looking up at the window in the door. "I kna nawt about no borglry," he protested. As I delved into my briefcase in reach for my pen, he suddenly moved, reaching deep inside the front of his trousers, raking around in his jockeys and produced a handful of £10 notes, instantly throwing them urgently into my brief case. He stared at me. I was in shock. I slammed the lid shut with the cash still inside then turned to see if the officer had seen me. I expected him to burst through the door and arrest us both.

"That's my own cash Mr Gibson," he protested: "It's NOT stolen."

For a split second I froze. I did not know what to do. I had stolen cash from a pub burglary in my briefcase. The police had not searched him properly on arrest but, in a knee jerk reaction and my heart thumping, I quickly opened my briefcase and threw the cash back at him: "I am not having that," I said under my breath and angrily as he scooped it up and stuffing it back down his pants. "The money is good," he said, "It belongs to me."

I did not believe him. He hadn`t worked an honest day in his life and the odds of him having the cash legitimately were higher than a one- legged man climbing Mount Everest without oxygen.

The officer had not seen us. I was lucky. I breathed again, jumping off my seat and banging on the detention door, demanding to leave. The police did not recover the money and legal privilege between solicitor and client prevented me from telling the Custody Sergeant but I refused to act for him again. The lesson: the client is my worst enemy.

*

Driving home that same night and recovering from the awful experience, I recalled a young female solicitor, fresh from university, taking instruction in the Newcastle Court cells. It was her first client and no doubt stressed. While taking his instructions the prisoner produced his driving licence and pressed it into her hand, demanding, "Keep that for me." She did not know how to deal with the situation and foolishly popped it in her handbag. The Custody Sergeant rounded the cell door, an expression of annoyance and a large hand extended, "Give me the driving licence back," he demanded of the prisoner.

"I Do not know what you`re on about copper?" he replied insolently. There was a standoff, staring eyeball to eyeball, then the Sergeant turned to the solicitor: "If he hasn't got it… you have," beckoning her to hand it over.

Blushing with embarrassment, she produced the driving licence and was frog marched up stairs to the Custody Suite and detained in a cell. Her client had sneaked the driving licence back off the custody sergeant`s desk and slipped it into his pocket, but only after a record in the property register. Given a stern warning, she was released but never again would she be allowed to visit prisoner's in the cell. She had acted naively, but not dishonestly. The police decided the incident was too embarrassing to have to explain how the driving licence ended up back in the prisoner's pocket.

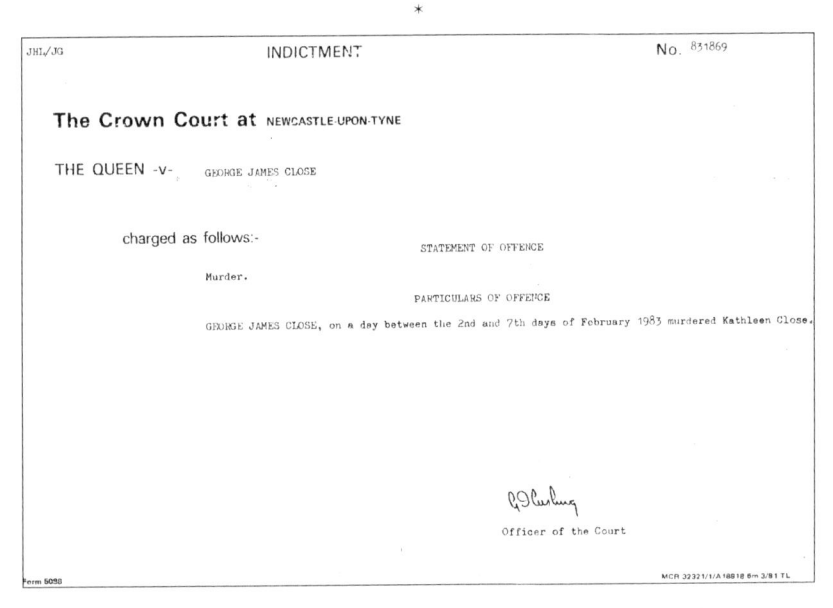

*

```
JHL/JG                    INDICTMENT                         No. 831869

   The Crown Court at NEWCASTLE-UPON-TYNE

   THE QUEEN -v-    GEORGE JAMES CLOSE

         charged as follows:-
                                     STATEMENT OF OFFENCE
              Murder.
                                     PARTICULARS OF OFFENCE
              GEORGE JAMES CLOSE, on a day between the 2nd and 7th days of February 1983 murdered Kathleen Close.




                                          G.J.Curling
                                       Officer of the Court

Form 5098                                            MCR 32321/1/A 18818 6m 3/81 TL
```

Wednesday 2nd February 1983 I attended the West End Police Station where George James Close, 32 years of age, arrested for the murderer of his wife, Kathleen. When I saw him in the cell, he could not grasp the seriousness of his predicament, chatting, almost jovially, about anything but the tragedy of the incident. He told me he had sold a portable television to a neighbour for £12 and the neighbour still owed £7. He demanded I go get the money back.

I spoke to the Detective Superintendent. "Her death was brutal and violent," he said. "They were at home lying on the floor, attempting to have intercourse." He described Katherine, "four feet eleven inches tall and weighing twenty- six stones." I visualised the scene.

9st. husband clubbed and strangled 26st. woman

WIFE'S LOVE TAUNTS LED TO DEATH

MRS. KATHLEEN CLOSE

"She was wearing her dressing gown… and nothing underneath. George was wearing a track-suit and they were both very drunk. She was up for sex, but George could not perform; probably the drink," The superintendent referred to notes, "she taunted him, saying she had had sex with other men far better than him and George lost his temper. He smashed a beer bottle over her head then dragged her lifeless body through the kitchen and down the garden path." I listened.

"Would you believe it Bert, he had started to dig a grave to put her in, but neighbours heard the screams and sent for us."

"Where is her body?" I enquired. "I may need a second post mortem."

"Morgue; Newcastle General"

Photographs of Kathleen pushed under my nose, of her naked body. I turned them upside down in confusion. I did not know what I was looking at. The photographs seemed to be out of focus. I thought I was looking at an over-grown tomato; then realised what a woman of Kathleen's size looked like naked.

53

I returned to the cell. George was rambling and confused, talking about his television, his neighbour. I wanted to discuss his wife's tragic death but couldn't get through to him. I wanted to know if he knew he was at the police station and the reason for his detention. Did he know he had murdered his wife? I promised to get the rest of his money, though he would not be going shopping for a while.

He appeared before Newcastle Magistrates' Court and promptly remanded to Durham Prison. I visited him there several times, occasionally with my barristers. We agreed we needed psychiatric reports. George was unable to grasp what he had done. This reminded me of my days at the Criminal Investigation College in Wakefield where a lecturer from the Home Office told us, "you must get to the murderer as soon as possible, and without delay, before he convinces himself he hasn't done anything wrong. The horror of his murder could blow his mind,"

George eventually began to open up and talk. A heavy curtain lifted, opening his mind to the horror of the incident. He broke down and wept tearfully relaying the occasion with bursts of regret.

He and Kathleen were lying on the floor in the sitting room. They had been drinking bottles of beer and cider and she wanted sex. George couldn't manage. "Too much drink," he choked.

She taunted him relentlessly of having sex with other men. He lost his temper and picked up a beer bottle, striking her over the head several times. George demonstrated. He swung his right arm high, pretending to bring the bottle down hard. He relayed the incident to me, minute by minute. It must have taken great strength to drag her down to the bottom of the garden. George was wiring, only 9 stone`s in weight.

"There was a lot of blood," he mumbled, "I used the cord from her dressing gown to tie her ankles then dragged her to the back door and along the garden path. Would have buried her," he admitted.

It took five burly police officers and two funeral directors to move Kathleen`s body into the hearse.

James Chadwin QC prosecuted. Mary MacMurray QC and Bill Hannah mitigated the circumstances, providing the Judge with several psychiatric reports.

George pleaded guilty to manslaughter on the grounds of diminished responsibility and jailed for five years.

*

My business was growing steadily. I was not in Premier Division with solicitors such as Bradley V Stephens, John Foley, Lewis Pearson and Gerry

Bass but my clientele was increasing by the day.

I made one of my regular trips to the West End Police Station and chatted with the Custody Sergeant. We discussed prisoners and bail and it soon dawned on me that many defendant`s would be released after charge if the Custody Sergeant had authority to impose conditions on their bail e.g. "do not return to your home," where he had assaulted his wife, or "do not go back into shops he had stolen from."

I wondered why only Magistrates` had powers to attach conditions on their bail. The Custody Sergeant often wanted the prisoner released from his station, but needed assurances the defendant would not go back to commit further offences or interfere with witnesses. Police were also losing front line officers kept off the streets to supervise the prisoners.

I wrote to the Home Office suggesting Custody Sergeant(s) throughout the UK, should have powers to bail prisoners with, or without conditions, where they felt it was in the interest of justice.

I am proud to say that every Custody Sergeant in England and Wales now has that authority, putting officers back on our streets and saving thousands of pounds to the taxpayer.

Chapter Six

An ex colleague, a traffic sergeant, rang me. He urgently wanted to meet me: "but not in your office, Bert; somewhere quiet." He had over fifteen year's police service. I wondered what it could be.

We met in a café out of town, his expression suggesting his world was about to end in tragedy.

"Got a big problem Bert," he said. I ordered two coffees. His hand shook as he took a sip, spilling drops onto the table.

"You're not taped are you?" He was paranoid, his eyes everywhere, including the door. I patted my pockets casually, "empty" assuring him.

"I think I am in big trouble."

In half whispers, he relayed his story.

He and his wife lived in a small village in Northumberland. They were being verbally abuse by a neighbour. "Every time we go into our garden she is watching us, cursing and swearing at us. I think she's mental." He finished his coffee.

"My wife couldn't take it anymore. She was so upset. This woman kept giving her two fingers and exposed her breasts to me in front of my wife. She was a bloody nightmare, Bert. We didn't know where to turn or what to do. I felt like jumping over the fence and breaking her bloody neck, but I'm a copper." I had never seen him so angry. "She told my wife I had slept with her, the lying bitch." He was near to tears.

"I was on patrol in the Rothbury area. I stop to check a lorry carrying scrap. I knew him. He had a record. We talked and he started to tell me his problems and, foolishly, I told him mine. I told him about my neighbour and he told me not to worry, he would sort it. "I would not have the problem anymore." He said. "I warned him about his driving and let him off. That was the end of it. I went on patrol and thought nothing more. I honestly did not understand what he meant when he said he would sort it" He shrugged his shoulders, "but two weeks later he stopped me and said a funny thing. He said," `You were working early shift last week?` "I said I was and he said," ` I didn`t know you left for work that early in the mornings`. "I didn`t understand what he was getting at. Then I got a shock when he told me he had been lying in the fields opposite my house and waiting for my neighbour to appear at her front door. He told me had had his gun and would shoot her"

I didn`t know what to say. The colour drained from his face.

"I was shocked, Bert. I really was. I didn`t think for one minute he was going to do that. My God, I could have been up for conspiracy to murder."

"What did you say to him?" I asked.

"I told him not to be so bloody stupid. I didn`t want him to do anything to her. I told him never to come near my house or my neighbour`s."

"So nobody got shot?" He shook his head,

"No thank God"

"I haven`t been involved in any sort of criminal conspiracy have I, Bert?" he was desperate for reassurance.

"I know him Bert. If he is locked up, I`m worried he might tell the copper I wanted to kill my neighbour. Just to get off the charge. What do you think?"

I gave him advice. "Have it out with your neighbour or move."

I heard nothing more and his career ended at full term with a good pension.

*

I always liked to make notes in my scrapbook of High Court rulings Stated Cases they are called, decisions from the God`s we lowly solicitors must follow religiously when representing clients. A sort of legal ten-commandments: rules to follow without question, but some, I thought, lacked common sense.

Possession of an Offensive weapon: i.e., someone found carrying a knife or bottle in a public place for his protection. The High Court decided that to secure a conviction the suspect must carry the item… to cause injury. Simple possession of the bottle or the knife to frighten is insufficient. Where, you may ask, is the common sense in that decision? If someone wanders our streets carrying a knife or a bottle or anything else for that purpose, and without good excuse, he should be convicted irrespective if he wanted to frighten or to injure.

The offence of: Going Equipped arises when someone is in possession of an article to burgle, steal or Commit Fraud. Maybe, a screwdriver or a hammer, with the intention to steal from an unattended motor car, but our learned High Court Judges have ruled that he cannot be convicted if he has already committed his illegal act… and was now on his way home… with the screwdriver or hammer in his hand. He is no longer going to commit a crime.

New fines imposed on convicted defendants. It is the Victim Surcharge, a fine by any other name, payable by every convicted criminal irrespective of the fact the offence may be victimless e.g, drunk and disorderly, urinating in the street.

Imagine the scene , our Learned High Court Judge sending a convicted murderer to jail for the rest of his life having to tell him, "You must also pay the victim surcharge" What do you think would the response? Probably a two- fingers salute as he headed for his prison cell.
"Sue me for it."

In the 19th century, our Learned Judges` would don Black Cap before sending the convicted prisoner to Tyburn to hang by a rope. Imagine the judge having to tell him to pay his victim surcharge then. "If I refuse to pay will you postpone the execution?"

In the 18th Century, the defendant would witness a far less tolerant judge than here in the 21st century. In those days the hangman`s noose was a regular occurrence for what we today would call minor breaches of the law. It was almost a fashion to send the prisoner to his grave for simple acts of larceny, (theft). Even the unlawful opening of a letter would end the offender's life and a plea for leniency from his Leaned Counsel fell on very deaf ears.

*

Whilst on holiday I would take my law journals for a little light reading, but to mumbling discontent from Anne and the children. "Put the books away dad. We are on holiday," I loved to read about the law and determined to be the best solicitor I could. I would have felt acutely embarrassed had I quoted law wrongly or law out of date and the length of sentences given always a concern. How often have we read criminals jailed for several years without mentioning the actual truth? That he will serve only half the sentence with further time spent on remand also discounted.

We trust our judge's to determine the correct sentence and its length, so why should the prisoner be released earlier? Did the Learned Judge make a mistake? He did not get the sentence wrong. No our politicians are to blame. They set the tariff and make the law, but one thing is paramount, the victim and his family should know the truth. Would we pay a builder £500.000 to build our home then let him off when he has only reached the ground floor? There is an agreement in society. A duty of care toward each other, to do no harm, breach of which results in punishment and the full sentence of the court must be served and not only a portion.

I have seen semi illiterate criminals; those who struggle to write their names, with the mental dexterity to calculate prison release dates almost to the hour; an ability to astound their former teachers.

A man convicted of cruelty to animals might be disqualified, from owning or controlling animals for many years or for life, yet he is able to return to his home: to his wife and his children without enquiries from social services. A propensity to do harm may not stop at only animals under his control.

On a lighter note, I do recall a woman solicitor relaying her story of trying to prevent an adoption order. She was unsuccessful and her client inconsolable. She decided to drive her home but on route switched on the car radio to hear, "Baby Come Back," a 1960's song recorded by The Equals. Her client was suicidal.

A conviction for dangerously driving a motor vehicle will automatically disqualify him for a period of at least one year, after which he can legitimately apply for a provisional driving licence and to re- take his driving rest. Until then he can drive on our roads legally but must display `L` plates, insured and be supervised like any other learner.

However, during the course of his journey, should one of the `L` plates accidentally fall off, he is deemed there and then to be driving whist disqualified.

The charge reads:

"That you drove a mechanically propelled vehicle whilst disqualified from HOLDING or OBTAINING a licence…"

This is clearly a fiction and the police, Crown Prosecution Service and the Courts know this. He is no longer disqualified, from holding or obtaining his driving licence. He received it lawfully from the DVLA. Now he is at risk of going to jail.

*

A Court Order introduced by our illustrious Government to keep persistent criminals out of jail. Known as a Community Rehabilitation and Punishment Order and used frequently, sometimes in abbreviated form. Imagine the hilarity of lawyers pleading with the Bench not to send clients to prison, but instead to impose a CRAP Order.

The offence of driving a motor vehicle whilst unfit through drink or drugs has, as its ultimate purpose, the desire to keep offenders off our roads. To stop them killing others and, on conviction, it is obligatory to impose the minimum period of twelve months disqualification. To reinforce our government's intent to keep death off our roads they quite rightly determined that on a second conviction, within ten years of the first, the defendant must be disqualified for a minimum of three years. The law is clear, it gives a strong warning, but the public may not be aware that in both cases the defendant can receive a substantial reduction getting him back onto the roads early. He must attend and complete the rehabilitation, training course. Listen to what bad boys and girls they have been then the period of disqualification reduced up to a third: in some cases a whopping nine months off his three year`s disqualification. Are we keeping death off the roads?

The law also allows the defendant to return to court and appeal the return of his driving licence after two years have lapsed and, if successful, he could have his driving licence returned to him after only HALF the period has expired. A five years disqualification reduced to two and a half. Should the defendant receive a prison sentence and a period of disqualification, the sentences run together. A prisoner could serve the period whilst serving his prison sentence and step into his car again at the prison gates.

A charge of robbery also troubles me. It is an offence so serious it carries a life sentence, yet the elements to convict are so ridiculous as to be farcical.

The law states:

"The defendant has to steal from someone and, at the time of doing so, and in order to do so, he uses force or the threat of force, on any person." Should the defendant inflict violence AFTER he steals, then parliament decreed that is not robbery. The violence must occur first.

Why? I will never know.

Think about it. The thief steals a lady`s hand bag. She attempts to stop him, to get her property back and he assaults her then runs off with her bag. This is not robbery, as the violence inflicted by the defendant was too late. Amazing? Yes. The violence occurred in the wrong order and, if arrested he would face a conviction of only assault and theft and a jail sentence measured in weeks not years.

Where a thief attacks someone then he drives off in his victim's car, he does not commit robbery. The events have occurred in the right order for robbery but our government has decided the offence is only assault and taking without the owner's consent (TWOC). It is not theft, but a joy riding, a name dreamed up by our news media. In America, it is Grand Theft Auto and the defendant goes off to jail before his feet touch the ground.

From time immemorial, our law has been at pains to assure the public that we are all innocent until convicted by a court of law but the charge of being drunk and disorderly convicts the defendant before he steps foot into court.

It states, "that you…on a certain date… were GUILTY whilst drunk, of disorderly behaviour`

Why bother going into court. As silly as a C.R.A.P. order

Chapter Seven

Monday 5th of July 1983, and the body of widower, George MacGill, was found by a passing motorist, his legs hanging over the edge of the pavement, his upper torso hidden under bushes only yards from Albion Row, next to the Byker Wall where he lived. 62 years of age and a former shipyard worker and Royal Marine, he lived alone in his one bedroom flat and described by neighbours in news reports, "as a happy go lucky man who never caused any trouble. He wouldn`t hurt a fly."

George MacGill, visited the Plough Pub at Wallsend most nights travelling by bus, but a neighbour said, "He usually got off the bus one stop early, because he enjoyed the walk,"

It was suspected that his attacker may have hidden in wait for George and by mid- night the police had set up their Serious Incident Room in Clifford Street Police Station and asking for information. Joe Bulch, would head the murder hunt with detectives buzzing the area calling on suspects and looking for clues, all the usual enquiries, checking criminal records for possible suspects.

Dr. Harischandra Ranasinghe, Home Office pathologist, confirmed MacGill had been attacked with a blunt instrument sustaining head and bodily injuries, a broken breastbone, five ribs cracked and a ruptured heart. Death, he would confirm, was due to blood inhalation.

Within two days William Bright, 30 years of age, and an unemployed warehousemen living at St Lawrence Square, Byker, had been arrested and charged with MacGill`s murder.

When I met Bright in the police cell, it was patently obvious he was mentally disturbed. I would need psychiatric reports. He appeared before Newcastle Magistrates` Court and remanded to Durham prison where I would take his instructions, noting his antecedents, family tree and his life history, ready to brief my legal team.

On the 13th March 1984, Bright appeared before Newcastle Crown Court where Mary McMurray QC, explained to Mr Justice Cullogh that MacGill had made sexual, repugnant, advances to Bright.

Nigel Fricker QC, for the Crown, told the judge that only six days earlier, Bright had also attacked a 72 years old man, punching him in the mouth and leaving him dazed and injured, lying on the ground. A witness heard Bright shouting: "Don't call me a puff again," and on the night of the murder, Bright also attacked a 62 years old man, punching him in the face and kicking him as he lay on the ground.

Miss McMurray QC described Bright as a lonely man who had suffered a long history of mental disorder brought on by the tragic death of his mother in 1980. "That is when his strange behaviour began," she told the Judge.

William Bright pleaded guilty to murder. He received a life sentence, and I hung up another indictment on my office wall.

*

Two days following Bright's life sentence I was back in the real world dealing with routine thefts, burglaries, assaults and offences of public disorder. A 15 years old boy was detained at Market Street Police Station, one of six seen carrying a half size pool table outside of St James' Park football ground. He was the only one arrested.

During interview with the police, he bragged how they had gone into Fenwick shop, Northumberland Street, climbed to the fourth floor and decided to steal the pool table. In front of several members of staff, they carried it down four flights of stairs and out of a side door, without being challenge. He arrogantly boasted of their success, carrying it head high through the city streets.

"It was my idea," he bragged. "If the copper hadn't stopped us I would have had it in my bedroom." An officer saw them and they dropped the pool table and scattered.

The boy boastful admitted his theft, smiling impudently at the officer for being cunning, even referring to one of the gang as "Vegy." When asked to explain, he said, "Because he's the stupidest kid in Newcastle" The Officer interjected:: "That's odd. You call him Vegy. but he got away and you were arrested"

*

Time allocating to attendance at court was always a problem. So many clients to see at the same time but at court's miles apart. Often I had to travel to three and sometimes four court's in one morning. I found it prudent to attend the court farthest away first, which meant travelling in my own time and before the court sat at 10 am. Usually to Alnwick, Hexham, or Chester Le Street, in the hope my client would already be there on my arrival so could deal expeditiously with his case then jump into my car to my next court, begging the usher for an early slot, then a sprint into Newcastle where angry and sometimes threatening clients awaited. I was living on a knife-edge knowing at any court I could face delay, seeking forgiveness from the client for being late and promising it would not happen again… with fingers crossed.

*

Anne worked a few hours each morning but I needed staff. Kath Smith, answered my call. She said she would help for a month only but stayed on as my personal secretary for over twenty-two years, my oracle and trusted centre of command, controlling my files, dairy and keeping on top of my heavy case-load. I don't know what I would have done without her.

Stephen Graham joined as a partner to cover family and to help me in the courts when needed. A good advocate, he and I became close friends and I owe him a great deal of thanks for his loyal support.

We took on another typist and then a junior to assist with the office administration: making cups of coffee, preparing post, delivering letters around town and banking. A very pleasant, happy young girl, she soon settled and the office ran like a well-oiled machine, but I was approached by a member of staff, "every time I go into the junior`s room, she smells," she held her nose in the air, "B.O." Like all good cowards, I decided this was not a matter for me and ignored her complaint hoping it would disappear. Later that week the typist marched into the junior`s room and took it upon herself to speak direct and abruptly; no holds barred, with the consequences that our junior left in tears, never to return.

I checked the junior`s room. There was a strong lingering pungent smell leading me to an old Bakelite double socket in the corner of the room. It was overheating and causing the stench. The junior was innocent.

*

Late afternoon, 27th July 1984, I was at the West End Police Station where a tall, slim young man, Mohican style haircut and dressed like a punk rocker was under arrest for murder. His heavy black hob nailed boots and thick studded belt were lying tangled on the floor outside the open cell door. A police officer was on suicide watch focusing his attention on my client`s welfare, hoping he would not try anything stupid, like banging his head off the walls or trying to top himself. It is always a concern to the police that someone in that situation would try self- harm.

The sight of Rodney Phillip Cobbold would frighten most people, particularly the elderly. His hairstyle, the way he dressed, a mix of rock, mod, and eccentricity was something to see. I worried my kids could end up looking like that.

He gave me a harsh stare then a look of confusion. I introduced myself and we chatted. I wanted to gain his confidence, promising to help, and reassuring him, I was on his side.

"I understand you have been arrested on suspicion of the murder of Ian Dunwiddie?" He stared as if hearing the charge for the first time. We spoke

Punk stabbed sniffer — Q.C.

By MIKE SNOWDON

Teenager denies murder near pub

PUNK rocker Rodney Cobbold stabbed a glue-sniffer to death after a night of drinking, a court was told today.

Durham Crown Court heard how Cobbold, 19, of Wellington Street, Gallowgate, Newcastle, lunged with a knife at 18-year-old Ian Dunwiddie, stabbing him through the heart.

Cobbold pleads not guilty to murdering Mr. Dunwiddie, of Colby Court, Rye Hill, Newcastle, who died outside the Black Bull pub near St. James's Park.

Mr. William Crawford, Q.C., prosecuting, told the court Cobbold drank bottles of cider and 20 cans of lager, sharing the drink with two people who shared the flat in Wellington Street with him.

He said all three—Cobbold, fellow lodger Steven Hogarth and John Hines, tenant of the flat—were joined later in the evening by two other people, Gordon Flanagan and Sharon Skellern.

At about 11.30 p.m. on July 26 last year, Mr. Flanagan and Miss Skillern were escorted out of the flat, down an alleyway by Cobbold.

They then came across three young men who had bags of glue with them. One of these was Ian Dunwiddie.

Mr. Crawford said Cobbold, who was dressed like a punk rocker and who had a studded belt and a Mohican hairstyle, was then offered two bags of glue to sniff.

He said Cobbold and one of the other glue-sniffers started to stare at each other and words were exchanged. It was then that Cobbold ran back to his flat and took the knife from a drawer in the kitchen.

Mr. Crawford alleged that two of the glue-sniffers ran away from the scene in an alleyway near Wellington Street, leaving Ian Dunwiddie talking to Mr. Flanagan.

It was then that Cobbold ran up and stabbed him through the heart. Mr. Dunwiddie staggered away, clutching his chest and collapsed on the pavement outside the Black Bull pub.

Mr. Crawford said Cobbold then stood outside the pub brandishing the knife in his right hand and the belt in his left.

He said Cobbold was then seen by two members of the Northumbria Police Vice Squad, who were in the area at the time and approached him.

"Cobbold's reaction was to swing his belt and wave the knife at the officers. He lunged at both of them with the knife and they backed off. He then smashed a window in their police vehicle.

"Ian Dunwiddie was still lying mortally wounded at the edge of the road," said Mr. Crawford, who added that Cobbold was followed by one of the police officers as he returned to his flat where he was arrested.

Proceeding

---

of his arrest but decided now was not the time to tell him his life was about to change, forever.

I spoke to Acting Chief Inspector Lance Davison, in charge of the investigation, who disclosed the facts: Cobbold had been drinking all night at his friends flat in Wellington Street. He and his two pals had emptied several bottles of cider and at least 20 cans of larger. Cobbold had staggered from the flat and, by chance, he met three glue sniffers, including Ian Dunwiddie. Glue melting off his lips, his eyes glazed, Dunwiddie held out two bags of glue and rocked rhythmically. He offered Cobbold. a bag full of glue. They argued, why we will never know, but Cobbold turned back to the flat and rifled through the kitchen drawers, returning with a knife and waving it high, making threatening and prodding motions toward Dunwiddie.

Dunwiddie's pals were terrified and scattered. Cobbold plunged the knife deep into Dunwiddie's chest.

"It would be like a hot knife cutting through butter," the pathologist would later tell H M Coroner. "People don't understand how easily a knife can go through human flesh."

Bleeding heavily Dunwiddie staggered a few paces toward the Black Bull Public House at the corner of Stanhope Street and Barrack Road, where he collapsed and died.

The taxi driver and two police officers saw Dunwiddie bent over and lying awkwardly on the ground. The two police officers were giving first aid when Cobbold approached, the knife held high, his studded belt now wrapped tightly round his hand. He flashed the knife and chased them off back to their police car. The officers called for urgent assistance while Cobbold smashed the car windscreen then wandered off back into the flat and arrested.

The Scenes of Crime Officer took his usual photographs and collected blood samples unknowing the trauma awaiting. The Scenes of Crime Officer also called Cobbold. He had been collecting samples that would convict his own son.

Cobbold remanded to prison and, on 5th March 1985, he appeared before Mr Justice Taylor at Durham Crown Court where he tendered a plea of not guilty. There would be a trial.

Cobbold would admit to stabbing Dunwiddie but he argued for an acquittal that he did not intend to kill him.

William Crawford QC, for the Crown, outlined the facts of the stabbing and Cobbold gave his evidence to the jury. Miss McMurray asking him, "Do you accept the knife you had in your possession caused the wound from which Dunnwiddie died?"

"Yes" he admitted, "I didn`t mean to kill him. It is not something to be proud of, that I caused his death. The next thing I remember being near the Black Bull Pub and seeing Ian lying on the ground"

"Why did you have the knife?" she asked.

"I hadn`t meant to get a knife. I just wanted something to make him go away." His head dropped, he sighed: "I think I went mad."

It took an hour and forty minutes for the jury to return a guilty verdict, Mr Justice Taylor imposing the only sentence available for someone of Cobbold`s age. "Detention for life"

I pinned the Indictment to my wall.

*

My client, a young man in his mid-twenties had a drug problem and many convictions. He often promised to stop, but never did. He was found dead in a boarded up flat in Gateshead, the Coroner concluding death caused by an over doze of illegal drugs.

I had my suspicions, but no evidence, that he may not have taken his own life, that his death may have been unlawful and at the hands of others. He often talked of his involvement with dangerous people. He hoped one day would kick the habit.

"It's ruining my life, Mr Gibson, but one day soon I will stop"

A drug addict suddenly found dead. On the face of it, the cause was obvious: over doze.

But, he lived in the West End, and died in a derelict flat in Gateshead. He told me he was having problems. "Heavy people have fallen out with me, but nothing I can't handle" he said.

He may have been in the flat with others, sampling drugs. Maybe he injected a bad batch… maybe his suppliers forced him to inject a large amount, we will never know.

The pathologist concluded death was due to an over- doze, the Coroner recording misadventure.

"When people take illegal drugs," the Coroner announced." This can happen."

His family invited me to attend his funeral. I cleared my diary for that afternoon and stood at the back of the crowd as his coffin was dropped into the ground, listening to the vicar's eulogy and the wailing from family and friends. "A young life cut short by drugs" was the theme.

I turned to walk away, but several men surrounded me, borstal spots strategically placed on cheeks and 'thug' written all over them.

A burly rough neck his arms like Popeye, reached out a callused hand and pumped mine: "thanks Mister," he said with a toothless smile, "you done a good job."

I was the only one present wearing a suit, tie and polished shoes. He thought I was the funeral director.

*

I had gained much experience investigating and defending murderer`s and my office filing cabinets full. Work was rolling in and, with the support of my barrister`s, Mary MacMurray QC and Bill Hannah, I had the best legal team in the country. It would only a matter of time before they were both elevated to the Crown Court as a full time Judge and then we would have to say goodbye.

I felt comfortable in the magistrate`s court and work became more routine.

Having gained a reputation over the years for fairness and honesty, I received a call from the Northumbria Police. Ray Mitchell, Chairman of the Police Federation invited me to be their Federation representative, to represent police officers who may have got themselves in trouble. I accepted with honour. I would now be a frequent visitor to Police HQ and given access to privileged areas and information and spent many hours representing officers during caution interviews.

*

As the Police Federation Solicitor I frequently attended Headquarters and on this occasion to represent a Detective Sergeant who was also a witness about to give his evidence in an on- going Crown Court trial.

The complainant was one of the defendants at the trial. He was losing the case and did not want to go to jail again so invented the complaint to cast doubt on the prosecution.

His interview was under caution and conducted by a senior officer from Complaints and Discipline but it was soon apparent the complaint was without foundation and made to discredit the officer. The investigation complete I asked Federation to hold my hand written notes until the conclusion of the trial in case my office burgled. The jury convicted the three defendants and sentences ranging from 8 year to 12 years handed down. Now it was the Detective Sergeants turn. He walked to the dock and pressed a business card into the defendant's hand with the words: HAVE A NICE DAY

*

I attended Gosforth Police Station. A young Probationer Constable was under suspicion of causing criminal damage to a motor car. The officer would be interviewed by Superintendent Alistair Winn an excellent detective and my former colleague. I knew Alistair would cover all the bases, gather the evidence and be fully prepared. I had to act quickly.

I introduced myself to the constable. He was drawn and pale and trusted no one, particularly me, a stranger. I had to gain his confidence but I had an edge, being an ex- copper, and he slowly opened up. We had an advantage. My client was honest and trustworthy, a change from the usual suspect.

I worked on the premise he would not do anything illegal. There had to be an error somewhere, maybe a confused witness: something taken out of context.

I talked and he listened but unwilling to discuss the incident which brought him under suspicion but, eventually the story filtered through.
He had been on nightshift, panda patrol, and covering the Fenham area of the West End. At 2:00, in the morning he spotted a car drive passed with four adult males inside They saw him and took off at speed. He gave chase through an estate, suspecting they were up to no good or carrying stolen gear. The car careered along back streets where it was abandoned, the four occupant's disappearing into the night. The officer checked the car. The doors locked: "I thought it was stolen. I did not want it driven away."
The Superintendent had told me the Officer seen to burst the car tyre with a penknife. The officer first denied this insisting: "I did not have a knife," but I did not believe him. I put it down to stress and the thought of losing

his job.

"An elderly lady has made a statement," I told him. "She saw you drop a knife down the kerbside drain." He did not answer. I understood his concern, but I did not want to challenge her evidence in court; that would be a mistake. I would lose. Her evidence would be credible, honest and believable.

"Why should she lie?" I pressed him. "Why did you burst the car tyre?"

Time was short. The Superintendent was waiting. I pressed again and he confessed.

The owner of the suspect car had a long criminal record and it was obvious to me he had set up this young copper and now demanding compensation for the slashed tyre. I could not let that happen.
I told the officer how we would deal with it. We were ready for the interview.

The Superintendent questioned him and we explained the events in detail. "I believed the vehicle was stolen" he said, "I had to detain it in case the thieves returned. I believed the only way to secure the car was to burst a tyre" The superintendent made notes. "I did put the pen knife down the drain."

"Not what I would have done" Superintendent Winn said, "but your decision to stop the car to investigate was right. I believe the damage you committed was lawful and cannot be criticised." Alistair was satisfied. The officer could resume his duties.

"The incident is no different to an officer forcing entry to a house in search of drugs." I added. "They both acted in the execution of their duty," There was no criminal intent and the matter proceeded no further. The officer left the station with his head high, but a stern warning to remove the rocker- arm next time.

Chapter Eight

It was 3rd December 1884. I had been a solicitor for only a few short years but had represented more murderers than most solicitors qualified for thirty years.

John Oliver Pink, 37 years of age, a married man, arrested for the murder of schoolteacher Paul Yendall.

I arrived at Wallsend Police Station mid-afternoon to Mr Pink. As expected, he was angry: "The police refused to help me," he told me in a loud outburst of grief. I calmed him, told him I was here to help. It was a tragic incident; the last thing he expected from an otherwise uneventful weekend.

He and his wife, Nancy, had allowed their 15 year's old daughter to stay at her girlfriends house, the Rowe family, but what they did not know was their daughter was having an affair with Paul Yendall and they had arranged to spend that weekend at his home in Sunniside, county Durham.

Mrs Pink rang the Rowe family, to say goodnight. Mr Rowe took the call.

"Your daughter is not here."

Mr Rowe spoke to his daughter and secret was out. "She is staying with the school teacher their daughter shouted."

Mr Pink hurried to the Rowe's home. He needed to know what was going on.

"What's that teacher doing to my daughter?"

"I tried to calm him." Mr Rowe later told the court, "His reaction to the news seemed like 'shear shock' and he was behaving in a strained manner, his anger steadily rising, then he exploded."

"I will cut Yendall's throat," Mrs Rowe said in a statement, "He was shouted angrily: 'I will stab him in the heart; KILL him'.

"He was out of his mind," Mr Rowe told the jury.

Mr Pink rang the police, distressed, out of his mind with worry, demanding his daughter be brought home, shouting and threatening to rip the teacher`s heart out unless the police did something. The police were unsympathetic. The recording of their conversation confirmed when the officer told Mr Pink he could not demand the Police do anything. Then, almost belatedly, the officer agreed he would get someone to attend… as soon as an officer became available.

I understood Mr Pink`s feelings when he heard the response; any parent faced with such news would be traumatised.

"I needed help," he said to me. "The cop didn`t give a damn."

"I had to get my daughter away," he protested, "That man abused his position… a bloody schoolteacher… and the police wouldn't help… I grabbed my fishing knife and called a taxi and headed for Sunniside"

I listened as he relayed the journey to Hole Lane. It must have been the longest journey of his life, praying he would get there in time, every mile a nightmare, thinking of Yendall with his daughter.

Unknown to Mr Pink, two officers were at Hole Lane enquiring of Yendall. They were to patrol the street. Stop Mr Pink getting into the teacher`s house, but they had not been given Pink`s description. They were in Yendall`s lounge asking probing questions when Pink knocked at the door.

"Yendall insisted she was not there," the officer told the court.
Pink was allowed to enter.

"He seemed, cool, calm," The officer told the court. "I thought he was a friend"

Pink walked into the sitting room and lunged at Yendall.

"I thought he had just punched him in the chest. I didn't see the knife," The officer said in tears.

Yendall clutched his chest, staggering into dining room where he collapsed and died.

"Pink then went wild," the officer told the court. "He was so very angry. Out of control"

Mr Pink's daughter was later found cowering in a wardrobe upstairs in the bedroom.

Pink appeared before Gateshead Magistrates' Court I made an application for his release on bail. "He is a hardworking, honest, family man, without a blemish on his character," I said. "He is the victim." I pleaded, "Yendall was the author of his own tragic death; a trusted teacher, with the responsibility to look after children in his care, not to abuse them"

The Magistrates' were sympathetic but remanded Pink to Durham prison where he would remain until the date of his trial.

At Newcastle Crown Court, he pleaded guilty to manslaughter on the ground of provocation. David Robson QC, my defence counsel, advised the High Court Judge there was no need for a lengthy trial.

Mr Pink received the sympathy of the Court, the media and the press and given a prison sentence of four years. He would only serve half.

There were no winners. Yendall a married man had a wife and two children. He had sent them to Scotland.

When I arrived home that evening, a reporter was in my lounge relaxing. He asked for an exclusive. He offered to pay just to speak to the Pink family; to get their side of the incident.

I declined, inviting him to leave. This tragedy was not for profit. Many years later I discovered the school teacher was distantly related to me, on my mother's side.

*

I was moving into the premier division and decided I needed to broaden my client base to include other areas of work such as house purchases and sales, a lucrative area.

Peter Ross, a legal executive and expert in property law, joined me to head up my conveyance department. He had several contacts with members of building societies, banks and the insurance sectors and, in short time, his department was making a healthy profit.

Steven Graham was also doing a great job looking after our matrimonial clients, dealing with issues of divorce. He had an excellent bedside manner, sympathetic and understanding but I did not know just how meticulous he could be.

"The women always break down at some point during instructions," Steven said with a smile, "and during that time, when they are upset and crying, time is wasted. So I move her file to one side and concentrate on another until she has sufficiently recovered to continue."

That is what I call time efficient.

*

1984, a dry sunny month in July, Terry Warren, 19 years of age, was at home with his father when he argued and then beat him to death with a chair. A violent and brutal death, psychiatrists confirming Terry Warren was mad. For many years, Terry had walked the streets of Newcastle unsupervised. Care in the community, we call it. Give the patient a handful of pills and show him the door. You`re on your own and problem solved

Only Terry needed constant supervision. He had problems remembering what day it was and often forgot to take his tablets.

It was the July 30th when Terry finally lost control and battered his father to death, and why? His father had called Terry`s mother abusive names such as "useless." Terry`s mother was not there. She could not hear the words. They could never offend her as she been dead for a year.

Terry picked up a chair and struck his father over the head and face, crushing his skull, blood everywhere. The first chair he used on his father broke into pieces, so he picked up a second chair and finished the job. His father lay dead.

"Why did you do that to your father, Terry?" I asked.

"Not to kill him," Warren said, "to stop him calling my mother nasty names."

Terry was insane. Psychiatrists confirmed that fact. I referred to the McNaughton rule`s dealing with insane people. The rules to test insanity used for the time in court during a criminal trial in 1843 involving the murder of Edward Drummond, Private Secretary to Prime Minister, Sir Robert Peel.

McNaughton, the defendant, had shot Edward Drummond and for the first time psychiatric evidence admitted to establish a bench- mark for criminal insanity.

The Test:

'It must be clearly proven that, at the time of committing that act, the accused was labouring under such a defect of reason from disease of the mind, as not to know the nature of and quality of his act he was doing, or if he did know it, that he didn`t know what he was doing was wrong.'

The classic example given to law students and detectives at the Police College is of an accused squeezing the throat of his victim, throttling him to death, but at the time, believing he is squeezing an orange; obviously mad.

Terry Warren was mad. He had undoubtedly committed the act but, due to his mental incapacity, he was unable to form the malicious, wicked, intent necessary for a court to convict. Terry did not understand what he had done. He could not follow the court proceedings and given detention in a psychiatric unit (madhouse) without limit of time.

Maybe that is where he should have been before this tragic episode?

What do we know about insanity? We have all done stupid things, like sailing across the Atlantic in a bathtub or tumbling over Niagara Falls in an oil drum. But does that fall into the criteria of mental incapacity… or just stupidity.

Ian Rimmington-Hall (I love that name) a single, 24 year of age, was crazy, I have no doubt about that, but not, criminally insane. For some time he believed he would be attacked in his bed. He bought a shot- gun (illegally) and hid it under his blanket. He awoke to see his blankets moving and, in an instant, blasted several toes off his foot.

Police were soon at the hospital to see Ian nursing his throbbing foot: "where did your little piggy go then?" the unsympathetic detective asked, "Did the big bad wolf chop it off?"

He was charged with firearm`s offences and detained under the Mental Health Act. He was mad: was he insane?
Children also do foolish things, sometimes for what they perceive to be the right reason, but with tragic consequences.

A house fire in Aldwick Road, took me to the West End Police Station where I met sisters, Yvonne and Karen Albright, 18 and 17 years, both arrested for arson (setting fire to their home). The tragic story unfolded.
They had overheard their mother`s cries of distress. She wanted to move her family to a new home far away from violent gangs, drug addicts and perverts. The sisters took their mother`s troubles to heart and, many sleepless nights followed, until they hatched a plan to help.

It was after midnight when they crept downstairs to the sitting room where they lit a small fire on the sofa; watching it burn and then put it out. They thought the smoke damage to the walls and furniture would sway the council to rehouse them. Their mother would be happy.

It was after two in the morning. They took a walk down the street, chatting how their mother would be so happy when they moved house, then heard the sound of the fire engines, horn`s blasting and blue light`s flashing. It rushed passed and turned into their street. They followed to see their house ablaze, flames shooting up into the sky.

Their mother was stretchered outside, unconscious and put into an ambulance. She would survive. Their 14 years old sister died in hospital.
H. M Coroner expressed deep sympathy to the sisters. Social services rallied round.

A tragedy meant with honest intentions. The sisters would have to live with the memory for the rest of their lives.

*

The Newcastle Youth Court, West Avenue, Gosforth has three courts, one large and two small all dealing with young whippersnappers disposed to criminal offending and in need of guidance before they end up in jail, like most of their fathers before them. I am saddened to say I have represented three generations of the same family.

Lewis Pearson, a well-known Newcastle solicitor, and reputation as a jovial wag, was in Court One representing a fifteen year's old boy who had stolen a motor car. The Bench of Magistrates' were deciding how to sentence him when Lewis interjected, calling for a psychiatric report.

"Why?" asked the Chairman, "the facts are clear. Why do we need a psychiatric report?"

Lewis replied, "He pinched a Lada. You have to be mad to pinch a Lada."

I had a trial in Court 3. I would represent a boy sixteen years of age. He would appear with five other boys of similar age and identification would the issue of contentions. "It wasn't me. I wasn't there." The prosecution would tell the court the boys' were in the stolen car and the police pursued them. They dumped the car and ran off. The prosecution conceded the boy's' were not arrested that night. Inspector Ken Warrington stepped into the Stand to give his evidence. He would say he chased a boy who evaded immediate arrest by jumping over a 6 feet high wall.
My solicitor colleagues would cross- examine him. I had nothing to add.

"How do you know it was these boys?" my colleague probed. "it was midnight... the streets dark...the best you could see was a rear view as a boy ran away. You could not possibly identify the boy...you arrested the wrong one"

Inspector Warrington was a member of our Over Forty Police Football Team. I decided to have some fun.

"How high was the wall officer?" There was a noticeable silence, his eyes closing menacingly, his jaw set, an expression telling me to back off.

I persisted, "The wall was six feet high. Can you tell the Court, in your own words please, why you were not able to climb over that six feet high wall," I kept a straight face. He refused to be drawn. I resumed my seat. Saturday while changing into our football shirts and boots, I mentioned to our team manager: "I think the Inspector should have a fitness test, Tom, before allowing him onto the field."

Ken an excellent copper and destined for the highest ranks, grabbed a football boot, threatening to throw it at me.

He retired with the rank of Superintendent; a very distinguished career.

*

Sunderland Magistrates` Court has its own comedian in the form of Gerry Armstrong, an excellent lawyer, but a compulsive Jester; probably the only true court jester in the country.

"Why has your client failed to attend this Court?" the Chairman asked of Gerry.

"Your Worships, my client had a curry last night and overdozed. He was rushed into hospital in a Korma"

Another one of his absent clients, Gerry explained: "he tried attend the court. He was late and tried swimming across the River Wear. The river is 79 meters wide but he only has a 50 meters badge and he didn't make it"

I had the dubious task of visiting Sunderland Court, and hoped to avoid Gerry`s jovial wrath but, as I entered the court and slipping silently into a seat at the back, Gerry spied me and the game was up.

The Jester called out for the Court proceedings to stop with a cry: "Your Worships, we are in the midst of a senior member of our learned profession from the great City of Newcastle." I lowered my head and cringed as several solicitor colleagues and the Bench of Magistrates` turned my way. An expression of wicket intent in his eyes he asked that my case heard first and I was ushered to the front with loud applause and to my embarrassment.

"We can't keep our learned colleague from Newcastle waiting," Gerry announced in cruel tones and I quickly address to the court, then turned to face a line of solicitor advocates each one holding high a sheet of A4 foolscap paper and, like judges at an ice-skating competition, pretending to mark my performance. I got an average of 6 out of 10…not bad… and the Magistrates' accepted this short inconvenient pause with a smile, but I was determined never to return to Sunderland Magistrates' Court.

*

A Police Officer had been detained at Gateshead Police Station. A very rare event indeed and, as Police Federation Representative, I attended to speak with him. The officer accused of stealing cash from court fine defaulters and, if convicted would be summarily dismissed from the Force. The local press would have a field day.

It was imperative from the off, the incident should be hidden from the public domain and most certainly from fine defaulters who would have all sworn on bibles a mile high they had paid the Officer, with the loss to the court of thousands of pounds in compensation.

The Officer worked in the Summons and Warrants department at Gateshead Magistrates' Court. He would visit the homes of fine defaulters and collect payment or arrest them and bring them to court. The money he collected, however, he put it in his own pocket.

It was only a matter of time before his ill-gotten gains were uncovered, and that is precisely what happened when he took himself off on holiday. Another officer took over his work, visiting non- payers who all were adamant they had paid. Some could produce hand written receipts.

When the Officer landed back at Newcastle Airport, he was arrested and during his interview, he accepted responsibility, blaming heavy debts. He pleaded guilty when he appeared before a Judge at Durham Crown Court and received suspended prison sentence.

Later, a disciplinary hearing with his Chief Constable saw him summarily dismissing him from the Force, his reputation in tatters.

*

Anne and I decided to move house to Kirkley, three miles north of Ponteland. A beautiful five bedroom Detached set in three quarters of an acre of lawn`s and tennis court. An oasis of peace and contentment.

Paul attended the local school, securing a place at university, gaining a 2/1 law degree and then a tenancy at Durham Barristers` Chambers. Jane obtained several A level`s then joined my office, temporarily, to gain experience dealing with the public. She eventually fulfilled her ambition to become an Air Stewardess flying with Britannia Airways. Anne and I are proud of them both.

Chapter Nine

3rd March 1986, another routine day, so I thought, but by late morning, I was on my way to Gateshead Police Station. Elizabeth Veronica Lambert detained with two girls for the murder of Angela Hinds. Tracey Debra Lambert and her sister Julie Josephine Mackell would also stand in the Dock

I met Detective Inspector Rosebrough heading the investigation.

"A young girl fell from the 29th floor of the Dunston Tower," he said. "We suspect it was not an accident. We believe your client and the two others are involved."

I made my way to the cell. An officer was outside looking in. suicide watch. The light inside was dull and purposely subdued. Elizabeth was sitting awkwardly on the edge of the seat her shoulders rounded her thin legs crossed, one over the other. She looked like death warmed up. Her face gaunt eye's tearful. She looked much older than her age.

I reassured her I would do all I could to help. He trembled nervously, wringing her slim hands anxiously.

"I didn't know she would do that?" She said in a faint whisper, rubbing her eyes.

The defendants were long-time friends of Angela Hinds. Meeting up since school days to do what teenage girls do best: chatting about boyfriends, hairdo's and sharing intimate secrets.

Angela had a secret she dare not share. She was having a relationship with the boyfriend of one of her group and that was taboo, a cardinal sin, and if the truth discovered she would pay.

"But I didn't want her to die," Elizabeth pleaded, "Nobody expected Angela to jump out of the window."

Angela's secret, became common knowledge and incensed, the girls set off in search of her, through the streets of Dunston, with hate filled eyes and fists tight, combing their regular haunts; pubs, cafe`s, friends flats, and then, near the Cross Keys Public House they saw her and Angela knew the game was up.

She ran to the Derwent Tower, a block of residential apartments 29 storey`s high and known locally as the Rocket. Angela`s grandparents occupied an apartment on the top floor and she needed their protection urgently, pounding on the door and pleading to enter, her angry friends close behind. Grandmother put her featherweight shoulder to the door and held it closed. Grandfather ushered Angela into the kitchen, closing that door and holding it closed. There was no other way out.

The defendants soon alighted from the communal lift and began kicking and banging on the door, screaming abuse at Angela, threatening her with violence, demanding she come out.

The front door burst open and grandmother sent flying to the floor, chairs and furniture overturned.

Angela was terrified. Only grandfather and a locked kitchen door kept them away.

She climbed up onto the kitchen bench and pushed the window open, reaching outside and trying to grab hold of something high above her. She had to get away before the door gave way.

Angela was hanging out the window, reaching for something, hanging precariously. She slipped, lost her grip and fell to her death.

I wanted to visit the apartment, to provide my legal team with the best information.

Was this murderer, or a tragic accident?

Accompanied with Detective Inspector Roseburgh, we took the lift to the 29th floor, stepping out into the communal corridor and left a few steps. The corridor lighting was dull, the walls bare and in need of a coat of paint. I stood outside the apartment. The front door was wide open, the lower hinges broken off. The sitting room looked like a war zone, chairs upside down, ornaments broken, magazines scattered, across the floor. Dabs of white powder smeared the furniture. The (SOCO) Scenes of Crime

Officers had been busy dusted for prints.

I walked inside. It was eerily silent. The kitchen door was lodged tight against the kitchen wall, cutlery and broken crockery, cups and plates lying on the floor. I moved to the window and looked out at the blue sky, a gentle breeze filling the room, bird's chirping on a tree nearby.

"I want to look outside," I told the Inspector, "see how far she fell," as if it were not obvious.

He disagreed. He objected. He did not want another death on his hands. I insisted, buttoning my jacket and climbing onto the bench. He held me with a strong grip as I pushed my head outside, looking down at the contours of the building and the slabs of concrete on the ground, 29 storey's below.

It was a shock, even for me. I prayed she would be dead before she hit the bottom.

The Inspector pulled me inside. We took the lift to the ground floor, not a word spoken.

I dictated instructions to Kath: "copies please for Counsel."

A young girl lost her life, but was it murder? Counsel would consider.

Mr Justice Peter Taylor, a former pupil at the Newcastle Royal Grammar School, sat in judgement at the Kenton Bar Crown Court. David Robson Q.C, a formidable orator and criminal expert, would represent Elizabeth. My barrister addressed the jury. they listened intently to every word. You could have heard a pin drop.

I did not write down everything he said, but it went something like this:

"Members of the jury, picture the scene. Angela Hinds is behind the kitchen door on the 29th floor of the Dunston Tower. Let your imagination run. Let your mind be a video and play out the scene. The defendant's forcing their way into the flat, the door bursts open. Now, ladies and gentlemen, stop the action there and ask yourselves this question: Is it foreseeable that Angela Hinds would climb onto the kitchen bench and attempt to climb out of that window? Would these defendant's believe,

even for one moment, that she would do such a foolish thing?
The answer, members of the jury, must be, "NO."

The defendant`s were acquitted of murder but convicted of manslaughter, each receiving a jail sentence of three years.

*

The Law Society Gazette dropped through my letter-box. I flicked through the pages, glancing at current events, recalling my father`s comments: We each have fifteen minutes of fame during our live time." A column in the third page was interesting.: "Her Majesty the Queen, has been pleased to confirm the distinction of Queen`s Counsel," followed by a long list of barristers.

I could not understand why barristers only received such distinction. We have many eminent solicitors equally worthy.
I sent a letter winging its way to the Home Office, suggesting similar recognition for solicitors.

"Would Her Majesty bestow the title of Queen`s Solicitor?" I asked. Someone must have read my letter, because we now have solicitors similarly honoured.

*

9.15 am on a sunny Thursday morning in September and I drove over the Tyne Bridge heading to Gateshead Magistrates` Court with an easy morning ahead; one defendant to be sentence and another in custody hoping for bail. I would be back in my office by midday and catch up on paper work.

Anna on Court reception beckoned me over. "Kath wants a word." A new client detained at Gateshead Police Station for theft and I made my way to the detention suite.

"Do you own a caravan, Bert," he asked, marking my presence in the book. Funny question I thought, but nodded. "Yes I have a caravan parked near Rothbury."

"Then you cannot see the client" he scratched my name out.

"He stole your caravan," he smiled, "now you know how it feels to be a victim." He was enjoying the twist in the tale. A solicitor, representing the villain's had himself become a victim.

"We will need a statement from you." He pressed a biro in my hand.

He told me the traffic Cops had stopped my client on the A1 while towing a caravan. "Enquiries have confirmed it belongs to you" The Custody Sergeant was enjoying every minute

I slipped quietly into court and listened to Peter Farrier in full voice telling the Bench of magistrates' how they should sentence his client. "You can't send him to prison"

The Bench did not appear to listen, doodling and dozing off, disinterested in what Peter had to say. He paused, mid- sentence, and wandered to the back, taking up a position in the public gallery and started mitigating his client sentence again.

The magistrates' eventually realised what Peter had done, probably from the echo in the room, and protested.

"Well, you weren't paying attention to me down there, so I thought you might listen to me from back here."

His client did not go to jail.

*

The cut and thrust of over 40's football was a welcome distraction and gave me the opportunity to keep in touch with my ex colleagues. Although our team would never make the premier division, we had some success, with Tom Brown, an ex- professional footballer who played for Middlesbrough selecting the team.

Tom, a detective sergeant based at Gosforth, relayed a story of making door- to- door enquiries, trying to detect a robbery. He knocked on a door and the occupant, male, recognised Tom, pleading with him to go into the lounge, where a full size framed photograph of the Middlesbrough Football team adorned the wall. Tom, his hero, was in the photo.

Frank Billham our team centre back, played for South Shields; strong and brave, like his brother David, a kamikaze pilot, fearless and prepared to risk life and limb to score the winning goal.

Ray Urwin, jovially referred to as "the animal," held our midfield together tackling hard and taking no prisoners.

Billy Chater, our right- winger, was without doubt, the fastest man in the league. He was a professional sprinter running at Powder Hall track where big money changed hands. When Billy had the ball at his feet, no one could catch him.

Billy Wakefield, at 6ft 4 inches was always the tallest on the field, leading the attack and towering above the opposition, heading in goals for fun. He would swagger off the pitch bragging endlessly, "I jumped so high to score that goal I was air sick"

Our home changing room facilities were excellent, the playing field manicured, but away games were often less than desirable, having to change some days in the police van and then playing on ice or heavy snow. We were to play in Sunderland and had to change into our strip in a room on the first floor of a social club. We were prancing around semi- naked, pulling on short`s and socks, when a double decker bus pulled to a halt outside the large window and several women on the top deck gawked when they got an eye full.

We cautioned each other for indecent exposure then went out and won the game.

*

Anne and I were at work, Paul at school. Jane was upstairs alone in her bedroom doing what Jane does best; music blasting, hairdryer in full flow and nail polish splashed all over.

It was late morning when she heard a noise in the house. There was no one else at home. She opened her bedroom door and shocked to see two men scruffily dressed moving her way. She slammed the door closed and dived for the telephone, ringing 999, calling for the police.

Fortunately, the burglars ran back downstairs and across the ploughed fields.

PC Frank Billham, our centre half, arrived first to console Jane whilst police dogs followed footprints running east to the stream. The Scenes of Crime Officer was dusting for prints and taking photographs when Anne and I returned and quickly checked nothing stolen.

Three weeks later, I attend Morpeth Police Station as the Police Federation Representative where the Scenes of Crime Officer had been arrested for theft.

He attended a burglary at Tynedale Council Office`s where the safe had been forced open. He took several photographs of the interior of the safe then stolen items inside. He must have forgotten as he took more photographs of the safe now showing the items missing

"Not the brain of Britain, Bert" the Superintendent said, "The items are shown in the first photo`s" he pushed them under my nose, "but look now, they are not in the second?" He threw the photo`s across his desk. "Thieves, people who are dishonest, can be so stupid."

I visited the suspect in the detention room and immediately realised he had attended my home. Anne had been troubled about a missing vase: "it has just disappeared" she mused. "It was there, on the table, when we came home." Women notice these things.

"Odd" I thought "because the burglars ran out empty handed."

The Superintendent questioned him. "Do you have any other stolen items at home?" He shook his head but Force procedure demanded his house be searched and, having entering the hallway, several stolen figurines stood proud on his window- sill, .including our vase.

I had to withdraw, my position compromised but he appeared before the Crown court and received a Probation Order linked with medical supervise. He blamed heavy workload.

*

I took on more staff, mainly typists and Kath kept her finger on the pulse, recording meetings, arranging conferences and court dates. She pulled me out of the s*** more than once when I forgot to attend courts or prison visits.

I needed a break. I took my family off to Florida, leaving the business in capable hands. Our hotel was on International Drive, Orlando. I hired a big luxurious limo and we cruised to Disney World, Epcot, Sea World, Kennedy Space Centre and many other places. I sent a card to Kath and the troops back in the office suggesting I open a branch office: "Mickey and Donald said they would look after the clients in our absence."

A fabulous holiday and all too soon we were flying home, jet lagged, and back into the cut and thrust of court work. Our service engineer called to maintain the typewriters. He wanted to know who owned the business and spoke to Anne. She thought for a moment and then, with mischievous grin, said; "my husband, Bert Gibson, is the owner of the business… but I own him, so you better make the invoice out to me."

Chapter Ten

I was at Newcastle Magistrates' Court. I would represent a young man charged with an act of indecency. He was in his early twenties, young, slim, neatly dressed and had not appeared in court before but these offences were so serious, for him, there was a risk of prison.

The prosecution read the facts to the Bench: The defendant had attached a tiny mirror to the toe of his right foot then wandered into a large department store in Newcastle and followed women up escalators, pushing his foot forward, adjusting the mirror until he achieved the view he intended: looking up their skirts.

"Why did you do this?" I asked. He was ashamed and remorseful but could not tell me. His mother was listening.

"I was under pressure at university," he lied, "I thought I might fail my exams and my parents would be so upset."

I thought they would be more much upset at their son appearing in court with his face plastered across the headlines. The press and a gaggle of photographers were outside awaiting the result.

He also admitted using his mobile phone in similar fashion, dropping it at his side and clicking away. A woman was suspicious, turned and smacked him across his face then called the police who, on searching his bedroom recovered volumes of indecent photos. He obviously had a problem.

The magistrate's listened to my mitigation. He had made urgent arrangements to consult a psychiatrist and his previous history of good behaviour and university education swayed them not to send him to jail.

*

2:00 pm the same afternoon and I was in the custody suite at Wallsend

Police Station. A young man in his mid-twenties arrested on suspicion of murdering his estranged wife. When I entered the detention room, he was stamping around like a wild-man demanding his rights, insisting he wanted to go home.

"I have done nothing wrong," he shouted angrily at me, kicking the wooden bench in temper.

"You," he pointed a menacing finger, "you better get me out of here or you`re sacked."

I disliked him from the beginning. He thought if he shouted, loud and long, he would get his own way. "That attitude will not work in the police station." I said calming him.

The police interview would soon follow.

The Custody Sergeant told me they strongly suspected he had killed his wife; strangled her during perverted sex.

The fact`s disclosed: The suspect had met and married his wife within a few months of meeting her. Her mother protested, trying to stop the wedding: You don't know him."

They lived as man and wife in his flat in Lutterworth Close, Longbenton: a whirlwind romance. She thought she loved him but soon realised she had made a mistake and returned to live with her mother. The marriage was over. She would never go back to him.

He had other ideas and, by chance or connivance on his part, they met in the Forum, Wallsend, where he swayed her back into his flat.

"She was happy to come back home," he insisted but the police suspected otherwise.

"It was her mother`s fault," he snarled, "she hated me. She caused all this trouble," he cursed.

"She came back home of her own free will" he insisted, "I didn`t force her. She was happy." I listened, making notes, preparing for the interview.

"We had sex; the way she liked it. She liked me to take her knickers off and put them in her mouth. She liked me to tie her tights around her neck." He was enjoying telling me. I did not believe him. Something was wrong. His Adams apple was bobbing about, he could not look me in the eye, a sign of lying.

"We often had sex that way" he said, "lots of times, but she must have suffocated. That`s what happened…. she suffocated,"

He wanted me to approve, to accept his account. I felt uneasy but kept an open mind.

"A woman would not do those kinky things," I suggested to him, waiting for his reply. He would have to answer such questions to the police, but he was adamant.

Did the police have evidence? It happened in a private bedroom, behind closed doors. Forensic would be useless. He agreed they were together.

Two detectives questioned him for hours, insisting he had kidnapped her, forced her back to his flat and had intercourse against her will. The questions were heated and probing. I had to intervene to calm the situation.

"She was not a willing partner," the Officer insisted, but as I suspected, they had no, independent, evidence and their case was going nowhere.

"You killed her," they repeated, hoping for a response. "You strangled her with her tights," they hoped he would confess. They needed an admission.

"You stuffed her knickers into her mouth and choked her to death," they wanted him to make a mistake, say something that would help charge him. Without hard evidence, he would be free.

They put back in his cell to make further enquiries.

"The pathologist may show acts of violence: a struggle. "A young woman has lost her life…and he did it," they strongly suspected, but getting nowhere.

"A few hours in the cell might loosen his tongue."

It was late in the evening when I made representations. He had been in custody long enough. He was free to go, but with a warning, "don't leave town. We might want to speak to you again."

H. M. Coroner held his inquest, the press in attendance. The jury returned their verdict: 'Unlawful Killing' and the community were in uproar, threatening to attack him, beat him up. His face spread across the newspapers.

"I'm afraid for my life he told me. "I cannot walk down the streets without threats and abuse. I am not safe here: do something."

I rang the Police, asked them to calm the press, defuse the situation. "Charge him or make an announcement he is innocent."
They refused.

"There's no evidence to charge him…yet," was all they would say.

I wrote to the DPP (Director of Prosecutions) insisting my client be allowed a fair trial, to prove his innocence and pointing to the decision of the Coroner's Court. "He has been tried and convicted in his absence. The public think he murdered his wife."

The reply was short. "There is no evidence."

H M Coroner and his legally constituted Court have no influence over the police or the Crown Prosecution who made such decisions. The Coroner's Court was to show cause of death, not to find guilt and many years later, when the inquest was arranged to investigate the cause of death of Princess Diana, costing millions of pounds, I knew it would be no more than a costly exercise to appease the public. The police had made their decision. Their enquiry closed.

*

My next case was both hilarious and animated. A single mother summonsed to attend the Magistrates' Court: 'to show cause why her dog should not be kept under control'.

A Policewoman had called to speak to her son and her dog took an instant dislike to the Officer, biting her. My client denied responsibility and pleaded not guilty, demanding her right to a trial.

"It was her own bloody fault," she said, "coming in to my house, lardy-darr, laying the law down…who the hell does she think she is?" I did not comment.

The Policewoman stepped into the witness box and recounted the events in graphic detail, "the dog rushed at me, biting me on my posterior," she winced at the memory and, until that moment, our case was going our way, but my client suddenly jumped to her feet shouting, "you're a bloody liar… it bit you on the arse."

The Court ordered her to keep her dog under control.

Chapter Eleven

It was a dull, damp, afternoon in October1987. I had been a solicitor for six years and dealt with a catalogue of offences but my next client stood in the Dock at Newcastle Magistrates` Court, drugged up to the eyeballs and swaying rhythmically.

"What is your name?" the court clerk asked him. "Hey man, what name do you want? There`s a whole bunch of us up here," pointing a nicotine finger to his temple.

The Chairman ordered him out of the court until he recovered.

My next stop was Byker Police Station, where two men occupied separate cells. Both in early twenties and a long history of criminal convictions.. The Custody Sergeant gave disclosure: They had set about a teenage boy, knocking him to the ground and stealing his mobile phone. The charge would be robbery and a very long prison sentence.

On statement`s, the evidence was strong. The boy had identified them. However, at court, when I consulted the prosecuting solicitor, he told me the robbery would be dropped and replaced with a minor assault and theft. "The boy was afraid to give evidence" he shrugged his shoulder. The defendants received only a community order.

The defendants were both police informants. They were more valuable to them on the streets, mixing with active criminals, than in prison cells.

*

Mid December. Christmas festivities, and I arranged for my ex- police colleagues, probation officers, insurance brokers and banking personnel to come to my office and celebrate, with a drinks and sandwiches as a thank you for work passed my way.

PC Andy Ashwell, the Market Street jailer, popped in for half an hour enjoying the chat and then he asked me to follow him into our office toilets. I was aware of Andy`s idiosyncrasies, but being curious, I agreed to follow him inside where Andy closed the door. I wondered what he was going to do next, but he pointed at the door lock:

"Look Bert. That is an Ashwell lock. My great grand da invented that. It is very rare." He studied it closely moving the parts back and forward along the rasp: "Not seen one for years." He beamed.

I had never given it a second thought but it looked impressive with its ornate brass bolt and cog-wheel which, when turned, moved a disc advising the toilet was occupied or vacant:

"A work of art," he said with excitement, "patented in 1883. Other ones are displayed in the Ashwell museum."

Suitably impressed I promised to admire it every time I ventured inside then returning to the party

*

Monday morning. I would represent a young man charged with indecency on a PSV (bus). It was alleged he 0ccupied a seat behind a young girl and began gently touching her long blonde hair.

"It was creepy," she told the court. "Like a spider running across my neck"

My client admitted he sat behind her when there were vacant seats elsewhere but denied touching her.

I suggested she was mistaken. "It could have been a spider or the collar of your coat?" She agreed she might have been wrong. "Well, I did not actually see him touch me" she said, "So I suppose it may have been a spider." That was sufficient for me to cast doubt but, unknown to me, one of the Magistrate`s had acquitted him earlier in the year for precisely the same conduct, and this time he was not getting way.

Back in my office and pressing my back into my chair, I surveyed the world of Bert`s Law and the pristine set of Halsbury Statutes I bought from a second hand book- shop. They stood proudly in my glass cabinet with several family photos below them. Three rows of indictments now filled the other wall and I contemplated the murderous history behind each one, and their victims lives cut short the perverted, twisted, mind of a human being capable of inflicting such evil violence on another.

Are we inherently evil? I wondered. Do these people possess a soul? Were they born absent of the sense of forgiveness? As a copper, I saw the most appalling acts of violence but thought inside a human being there was a kind of switch that said anger goes this far… but no further."

The murderer may not have that switch: unable to show compassion or sympathy, only blinding hate.

My indictments were a constant reminder to me of the vile, inhuman, unmitigated violence one human is capable of inflicting on another. Lives of innocent people cut short during a fit of temper, someone swimming in a sea of drugs or alcohol or both. I have stood in the court as each convicted murderer bent his head in submission: pleading for mercy. Mercy denied his victim.

Nine indictments hung on the wall, one woman and eight men, each serving a sentence of life in prison.

The death penalty abolished, in 1969, with the passing of the Murder (Abolition of Death Penalty) Act, 1965. The last official execution took place at H.M. Prison, Durham on the 17th December 1958 when Private Brian Chandler, only 20 years of age, hanged for the murder of Martha Dodd.

Wednesday, 13th, July 1955, Ruth Ellis faced the hangman Albert Pierrepoint, the official executioner.

I was always worried I may represent and innocent man hanged, due to my incompetence. I am pleased I was not a qualified solicitor in those days.

As a detective, I found a way of dealing with murderer`s, people the public rightly abhor and demanded the harshest penalty, those intent on committing unmitigated evil. I enjoyed hunting them down and seeing them removed from society for the rest of their lives.

Occasionally, in the cauldron of the investigation, a detective may let a sick joke slip from his lips: "On holiday in Saudi Arabia I saw an Arab walking the street with both his wrists full of stitches: "he won his appeal."

As part of the Incident Team, I attended the home of an elderly woman brutally murdered. She lived alone in her bungalow south of the river Tyne and senior officer's quickly decided unlawful entry had been made via the front door. To preserve evidence they clambered in and out through an open side window, but forensic analysis confirmed that the same window had been used by the murderer. Fortunately, there was evidence left in abundance inside the sitting room to arrest and convict.

*

3.45 p.m. on a mid- week and I was ready to go home. I had been awake since early hours and struggling to keep my eyes open. I slid down my chair, my long legs stretching out from under the desk and almost horizontal. I was comfortable drifting off, when Kath popped her head round the door and I knew that smile; the twinkle in her eye, which meant trouble.

I sat upright, blinked several times and reached for a burglary file, pretending to read my rough notes scribbles down at Newburn Police Station at 4 am that morning when the Duty Inspector called me to attend an old Victorian terrace house in Newburn. It was still dark when I arrived at my destination to see several police officers surrounding the open door, one officer shouting aggressively at someone inside, "Come Out. This is the law." I spoke to the Inspector.

"Morning, Mr Gibson," he quickly outlined the situation. Deka, was inside the attic with one other man and refusing to come out.

The Inspector's patience was wearing thin, "I want this problem solved without injury to your suspects or my Police Officers" .He thought my presence might sway them to come out.

"We believe they screwed a house in Jesmond," he said as he pulled his cap forward over his head. "We need to get them out of the attic without anyone being hurt. Can you help?" I moved towards the front door where he pointed up the stairs to the first floor landing and to the attic cover.

"They have barricaded themselves inside the attic, threatening injury to anyone who goes near. You are my last hope, Bert, you might convince them to come out."

I climbed the stairs to the attic, adjusting my eyes to the dark shadows. Blood shot eyes stared back from a dirty face.

"Fucking, come near me you bastard and I will break your fucking face," Deka shouted. I recognised his voice. He was no threat. He was all bluster, probably shitting himself with fear. He was never a violent man. He would run away from his own shadow.

"It`s me Deka…" I shouted back, "come down," gesturing to him, "I will look after you."

There was a long silence then a period of recognition, "Is that ye, Mr Gibson?" his face lit up.

"Aye, okay Mr Gibson but keep them dogs away from is," he shuffled to the edge, "We`re cumin doon"

I was underneath as they dropped through the hatch, spraying dust all over my hair and on my shoulders, but they came down safely and without incident, then into the hands of the law.

At the police station, they sang like birds, admitting burglary and two further offences of theft. Their willingness to give themselves up, quietly, and without anyone getting hurt, swayed the Inspector to grant them bail. I would see them at court.

*

"Your next appointment is Mr Smith," Kath announced; not his real name.

"Wheel him in, I said," rising from my desk to greet a smartly dressed middle-aged man wearing a navy hand stitched suit, not the usual client who walk through my door.

I shook his hand inviting him to a chair. He took a cursory glance around the room.

"How can I help you?" I smiled, going into solicitor mode.

"The case will be dropped," he said in a posh, London, a trace of arrogance spilling out. His gaze settled on my family photograph taken at Sea World, Florida.

"Florida. Very nice been there," We then got down to business.

"This is going nowhere." He said, flicking a wisp of greying hair from his jacket and watching it drift to my carpet.

"I know nothing about your case, Mr Smith" I half apologised.

"You will have to explain it to me." He let out a mumbling tut, fixing a taught mouth. "I've been charged with obtaining £25,000 from my bank manager." Again, insisting the case was no more than an inconvenience to him. "It will go away."

He produced a crumpled piece of paper, throwing it arrogantly across my desk. I smoothed it. It was his charge sheet identifying an offence of obtaining money by a deception. He had to attend Sunderland Magistrates' Court. I made a diary entry.

"Won't be there" he said, "I'll probably be behind enemy lines." He crossed his legs, looking passed me out of the widow. I ignored his remark about enemy lines.

"Tell me want happened?" I asked, pen in hand.

"I borrowed cash from Barclays Bank. No big deal," he let out a faint laugh as if the whole thing was a joke, an irritation. "Nothing will come of it," he said, "I will get MI5 to pay the money back. This case will be dismissed when they realise how important I am."

He looked sensible and appeared to be normal, but was he a loony tune? The need for a psychiatric report ran through my mind. Someone inside the room had lost the plot… and it wasn't me.

I studied the charge sheet, thinking over my options. Could I get to the door before he went completely bonkers.

"This will end up in the Crown Court," I tentatively told him, not wanting to vex him. "You could receive a prison sentence; maybe two years." He didn`t bat an eye. My word`s going over his head.

"Tell me what happened. Then I can give you my legal advice and whether you should go for trial with a jury." I held my pen as a weapon should he lose control.

"I told the bank manager I had won some money," he grinned. "I told him I was waiting for a cheque for £75,000 but I needed the money, now, urgently. He offered to advance me £15,000."

A cunning smile crossed his face, "you see, he wanted me to bank all of my winnings at his bank… a feather in his cap…the problem is I hadn`t won anything; not a penny. A few weeks later, I asked him for another £10,000, promising him the cheque was on its way. He kept ringing me, asking questions. He wanted to see me, to discuss the loan, but I put him off with excuses. My aunt had died. I was attending a funeral. I was in hospital. I promised I would call soon. All lies.

He called the Police. I was arrested and now I`m telling you it will all soon blow away. I am VIP. I am too important."

"Let`s get this right, Mr Smith," I pressed, "you deceived the bank manager to believe you had won a substantial sum of money, which was a lie, and you have admitted all this to the police?"

"Yes, but I am definitely not going to jail… it`s not going to happen."

He leaned forward as if to share a secret: "I will be leaving the country on assignment." He glanced over his shoulder, expecting someone to slip into the room, and I knew he was barmy. I needed to get him out of my office.

"Why do you think the case will be discontinued?" I needed to hear.

"I am an International Spy." Could I reach the door and call for help? Was he carrying a gun? I regretted not having a panic button.

"Err…I will meet you at the court," I said ushering him to the door, quickly scribbling down…psychiatrist…a sandwich short of a picnic.

The day arrived. I was at Sunderland Magistrates` Court and heading for the Crown Prosecutor.

"Good morning," I said jovially, "I am representing, Mr Smith. I believe you are about to drop this case." He leaned close, sniffing the air, a sarcastic expression filling his long narrow face, "you on drugs?" He raised a questioning eyebrow. "Your Mr Smith is going straight to jail, do not pass go do not collect £200," he said throwing the file on the desk. "He is going upstairs… to the Crown Court where I expect he will receive a lengthy prison sentence" He ignored me, flicking through a mountain of files. I walked away. He shouted to me, "Your Mr Smith is a conman, and has been caught… end of story"

I found Mr Smith relaxing in the cafeteria with a frothy latte in his hand, "The case won`t be discontinued." I told him, pulling a chair up, "in fact the prosecutor is betting you receive a prison sentence." I looked for a reaction: did he understand.

"Whatever," he shrugged, "he`s wrong…. I am an International Spy."

Mr. Smith was committed to the Durham Crown Court and as he walked outside I watched for signs of mental unbalance, expecting him to blow bubbles or do a childish hop skip and jump, but he strolled up the high street, his head high and jumped onto a bus.

"No Aston Martin then?

Kath typed the brief for Counsel and sent it off to Chambers, including a few flavoured words of descriptive about our Mr Smith.

I attended Durham Crown Court determined to see this case played out to the end. It was interesting if nothing else. Would he go to prison?

I spoke to my barrister, "never represented an International Spy before, Bert," he smiled, "is he a fully paid up 007?" We shared the joke.

I looked over to Mr Smith. He was sitting casually across the hall, carefree, calm and disinterested. I worried. Had I done enough to prepare this case?

The main doors of the court shot open and all eyes turned to see a smartly dressed woman breezing in with a no- nonsense air of importance and VIP radiating from every curve. Hair scraped back and pinned with a butterfly clip, thick spectacles hanging off the cutest nose and a large brown envelope tucked under one arm I caught the bold printed words `Home Office as she climbed the stairs to administration insisting, " I must see the Chief Clerk immediately." flashing something small in the palm of her hand.

Mr Smith`s case was called into Court, the Honourable Judge tapping his fingers irritably.

Mr Smith was sitting between two prison officers in the Dock, the prosecuting Barrister about to address the judge with the facts but His Honour waved the prosecutor to sit announcing: "Stand up Mr Smith," I glanced to my barrister. He shrugged his shoulders. "What is going on?"

"I am told you are a very important man," the judge said, "Our Government has shown me certain confidential documents and I am therefore unable to send you to prison. I believe your services are required elsewhere…" he coughed, "Government matters. My hands are tied."

He asked Mr Smith to stand. "I will impose a 12 months prison sentence but suspended it for two years. You may go."

Mr Smith stepped from the Dock and mouthed to me: "Told you so." On our way back to Newcastle, we stopped for a coffee where, Mr Smith entertained us with a range of linguistic skills and an in-depth knowledge of the problems facing the far- east.

I asked his real name, "If I told you, I would have to kill you," he smiled but I did not know if he was joking.

I could not believe I had represented a Government spy.

Chapter Twelve

The sun high, a clear blue sky and I decided to take a walk along the quayside. A bit of ME time before calling into Moothall Crown Court where I had to make an application for bail for my client on remand in Durham Prison. A slight breeze was blowing from the North Sea up the river and I stopped to smell the aroma of smelly bits floating along.

When I left school at 16 years of age and took up my first job it was for the Newcastle Warehousing Co., Hanover Street, our offices high on the hillside, overlooking the Tyne. I started on £2: 60p per week as a trainee wage's clerk and book-keeper, an important part of my work being to walk along the quayside to the Customs Long Room (now Trinity Barristers' Chambers) where I delivered a very high valued cheque as excise duty. The payment would authorise the release hundreds of barrels of wines and spirits from our Bonded Warehouse to shops throughout the north of England. After three happy year's I left to join the police service.

9: 30 am and I walked up Dean street, cutting through the Side to St Nicholas Cathedral and swinging left towards the High Level Bridge and into the Mootall Crown Court where at 10:00am I had an application before the Judge for bail for my client lounging in Durham Prison. I had prepared the paper's thoroughly but knew my prospects of success were, slim to nil, as the defendant was facing another long stretch in prison for violence and torture. He would not be present at the hearing and I was pleased.

I wandered in to meet Counsel for the prosecution and ushered to the judge's private room, bowing regally as we stepped inside. His Honour was at his desk his Judge's wig lying dormant on one side flicking through the pages of my application. Raising his head, he nodded, inviting me to speak and I offered him a variety of reasons to grant bail at any moment expecting he would bring me to silence with a firm rejection. Oddly, the Judge was not hostile towards me in fact quite pleasant, allowing me to proceed to a conclusion. The prosecutor objected giving substantial reasons why he must remain in custody, the judge tapping on the desk rhythmically with his pen: deep in thought.

I worried. Was he going to grant my client bail? I had attended him at prison two days before where he expressed a strong intention to do serious bodily harm to the prosecution witnesses should they dare give evidence against him.

This played on my mind as the Judge deliberated then he announced, "I will allow him bail with the following conditions…"

I interrupted. Something I had never done before. "Your honour, I have done my duty to my client by making this application. Now, for the safety of prosecution witnesses and others, I must ask you to refuse bail."

There was long silence, the prosecutor staring at me in disbelief. I had breached my duty to my client, but I did not care. The death or serious bodily injury to a witness was not something I could live with and, as we were in `camera` (in private) without public scrutiny, I said, "Your Honour, my client intends to inflict serious harm to witnesses to prevent them giving evidence."

His Honour thanked me then ran a thick line through the papers, "thank you for your honesty" marking them "REFUSED"

I risked a complaint to the Law Society, probably disciplined, but I did not care. Maybe a bit of the old copper`s sense of justice stuck to me, but I would sleep at night.

No one was going to be hurt on my watch.

*

My desk covered in files and briefs` awaiting for my attention when I returned from Moothall, my mind on the issue of Mr Smith, our International Spy. Why had he called into my office I wondered? There were numerous solicitor`s offices between here and London and as he was so obviously well connected, he had the choice of thousands of solicitor firms. Then I recalled a phone call from a Detective in Special Branch and realised he had pointed, Mr Smith, to me because I was the Solicitor for the Northumbria Police Federation. I could be trusted.

*

Another day was closing. Shadows lengthening across my desk and I gazed with tired eyes out of the window at the cluster of birds pluming feathers and settling on the ledge for the night, my thoughts drifted to the 21st December 1979; the day that changed my life.

It was late afternoon. I was driving through Prestwick Village, near Ponteland, when I stopped outside of a public telephone at the roadside. It was very much a spur of the moment thing and, to this day, I do not know where I got the courage, but I dived into the kiosk, dialled a number and waited, heart thumping.

"Alan Henderson, Beecham and Lee, solicitors", was the response from a young lady pretending to be posh: "Can I help ya`?" a touch of Geordie slipped out.

"Err, yes,..err… can I speak to Mr Eric Lee… please?" I stuttered like a four year old.

"What`s it in connection with pleeeaaaase?" she enquired, "are yu a client?"

"No." I said, "Err…it`s a personal matter."

There was silence. I took a breath then a cultured voice spoke.

"This is Eric Lee. Can I help you?" I was through to the MAN and I almost dropped the handset.

"Err, Hello, Mr. Lee." I grovelled, "I am a serving Police Officer, a detective, with the Northumbria Police. I have a law degree. I am wondering if you have a vacancy for an Articled Clerk," my mind flashed to the hundreds of law students making similar applications and suffering a multitude of rejections. All excellent students, many with first Class Honours.

"Come in for a chat," he said, "I may have a place for you."

I replaced the handset, bewildered at his response, staring at the face looking back from the small mirror inside, a mixture of shock and surprise. I jumped into my car, pushed through the gears, my mind a kaleidoscope of confusion but at 3 p.m. the following afternoon I was sitting in the reception of Allan Henderson Beecham and Lee, Solicitors, Pink Lane, hiding behind an out of date car magazine, trying to calm my nerves, the rhythm of typewriters and slamming filing cabinets. Opposite was the face of someone who`s mug-shot was manifest in our Force Album as `active`, his eyelid half asleep, mouth open, hair matted and the smell of B.O drifting in the air whenever the reception door opened.

I studied him closely, then instantly realised I had to stop. `Don`t stare like that` I admonished myself. If you do get the job, you will have to look at people differently: through civilian eyes…not a copper`s`. Thieves can smell a copper a hundred miles away. Maybe we have an odour all of our own?

To my left a pair of blood shot eyes stared back. He had the expression of a violent man, just the sight of him scaring most people so I dropped below my magazine and turned the pages, pretending not to notice.

A confrontation in the solicitor`s office was the last thing I wanted. Eric Lee would not want me turning his client`s away or it would be a very short interview.

I listened with disinterest to girls chatting about boy-friends, hair doo`s, their nails needing polished and nights out, my eyes resting on the framed certificates on the wall of the partners announcing their admission to the Roll of the Supreme Court of England and I wanted my name up there. One day, maybe

"Mr. Lee will see you now," a voice rang out from behind a clattering typewriter, pointing me up a narrow flight of stairs. A light rap on the door then I stepped into a room no bigger than a Police Box. Mr Lee hunched behind a double fronted antique desk, a mountain of files on top threatening to cascade off the edge at any moment. He waved me to a seat, his diminutive frame rounding the desk with a welcoming smile, offering a friendly handshake.

He spoke enthusiastically of his morning's work and the good fortune of swaying the magistrate's not to send his client to prison. "He was lucky, Bert, he got away with it this time, but he will be back. Asking me to represent him again" he winked. No names given, none expected, but I was all ears, listening to his experiences in the court, hanging on his every work, but harbouring doubts.

Was I doing the right thing? Could I be an advocate? For the past 14 years, I had been happy to take his clients off the streets: put them behind bars and protecting the public. Now I was actually pleading with him to let me help keep the villains out and, strangely, I was excited. I pictured myself in the cut and thrust of court advocacy: the next Perry Mason.

I had checked out Eric's attitude toward the police. He had a good reputation and held in high esteem, his reputation for fair play preceded him. "He doesn't bend the rules" the Force Collator told me, "He plays with a straight bat."

Then it was my turn to be surprised when he reeled off my career to date.

"You joined the Police Force in 1964."

"Was it that long ago?"

"You passed your Sergeant's exams in 1967, your Inspectors in 1971" He was forming an opinion of me.

"You have been graded for immediate promotion and now you have a law degree."

How did he know all that?

"You now need only pass the Solicitor Finals, but that won't be easy." He said sizing me up: how I would look and perform in the Magistrates' Court. More important, how would his client's react to me…an ex copper. Would I be an asset or a liability, then we got down to business, chatting about my police experiences, my posting's and the Serious Incident Squad where I was one of a team of four detectives' dealing with murders, robberies and protracted crime.

"What can you tell me about linking evidence?" He queried. I suspected he knew the answer. He asked about forensic evidence and cross contamination and my answer`s, short but detailed, must have been encouraging as he pumped my hand, "When can you start?"

It was as simple as that. Everything happened in a flash. The very rare position of Trainee Solicitor was mine. All I had to do was sign the deed of employment, welding me to the firm for two years and that was it. My legal career was opening up for me and I just needed to grab with both hands, and I had not told Anne.

I worried about resigning and what my colleague`s would say. "What makes you think you could be a solicitor?"

I had doubts. Was I doing the right thing? Giving up a secure job; losing prospects of promotion, swopping a lucrative pension for the unknown. Could I pass the solicitor finals? Many far brighter than me had tried and failed, ending up lecturing or joining the civil service or armed forces.

9:00 am the next morning and I was back in Forest Hall CID office pouring over unsolved crimes my head in a spin wondering when to write out my resignation. What would be the Chief`s reaction?

The solicitors I had heard at court when giving my evidence of arrest: Francis Kidd, Clive McKeag, Basil Mellon, Colonel Philips, Eddie Hathaway, all skilled advocates. Could I be one of them? Time would tell.

I turned the pages of a report of an overnight burglary, my mind unclear, unfocused, my future unsure. Detective Ken Anderson was sitting at the other side of my double desk, his 6ft 4 inches frame filling the chair, his gruff Scottish accent calling out for someone to make him a steaming coffee. He reminded me of my days pounding the streets of Berwick and those men in skirts with tree trunk legs.

A large pot of steaming coffee sat on the desk and he fiddling with paper clips, flicking them across the room to the annoyance of others. I pondered my future. I would be throwing away 14 years of hard work and, with it, the prospects of promotion.

The phone Ken and I shared, rang. Ken stirred and picked it up. "Forest Hall CID" he said in a-couldn't-care-less attitude, then his expression changed, his voice humble, almost sycophantic, a nervous cough and shuffling awkwardly in his seat.

"Yes sir." He said in loud, subservient, Scottish tones. "I will be there at ll.30am prompt, SIR. Thank you, SIR." The rest of us listened as Ken dropped the phone, staring out of the window an overjoyed expression filling his rugged face. Suddenly he pushed his chair back, sending it crashing against the wall, jumping to his feet, grabbing his coat and heading for the door.

What was that all about? We all looked at each other bemused, the office in turmoil, detectives, who had heretofore prided themselves on knowing what was going on in the big world sat back in confusion.

Ken always laid back. Nothing short of World War three or major disaster would interfere with his morning coffee. We agreed all that phone call had to be important.

By 2:30pm, our questions answered, when Ken wandered in, three sheets to the wind, shirt unbuttoned, his tie wrapped across his neck, and stinking of booze. He dropped listlessly into his chair and with a hic announced: "Been promoted lads…hic… to Detective Sergeant,"

I was pleased for Ken. He deserved his promotion. He was a good thief catcher, but I was also angry. The Deputy Chief Constable had promised me the next promotion when I returned from university. Ken's success was the catalyst had made up my mind for me and I typed out my resignation, in triplicate, throwing it into the tray marked, Headquarters.

I did not receive a reply, no request for an interview, no plea to change my mind and, on a wet Thursday afternoon in December, I collect my personal items and walk out of the office for the last time.

*

Kath brought me back to reality: "The cassette tape has snapped," Instructions recorded over the last two days were lost. I would be working late.

Chapter Thirteen

Thomas Henry Wolens murdered Joyce Liston. It happened on a sunny Saturday afternoon in the bustling Newcastle City Centre. The circumstances were tragic but preventable but no one, not even the police, came to her rescue.

Saturday 15th August 1987 and Thomas Wolens, a 34 year's old vagrant, befriended Joyce Liston a 58 years old care worker as she laid flowers on a family grave in St Andrews, Newgate Street. Having placed her flowers on the grave she sat in quiet contemplation for a moment then Wolens approached striking an unwarranted conversation. Joyce chatted for a few minutes then made her way alone through Low Friar Street to Marlborough Crescent, intending to return to her home in Middlesbrough. Wolens followed, engaging in conversation, following her through the crowded streets. At Marlborough Crescent, Joyce stepped into a café, probably in the hope of ridding herself of him, but Wolens followed her inside sitting at her table. She may have been too frightened or embarrassed to seek help.

Joyce crossed the busy road, descending the stone steps into to the lady`s public toilets, passing women going in or coming out. Wolens followed, ignoring the verbal protests.

Joyce entered a cubicle. Wolens pushed his way inside, holding the door shut with the sole of one foot and began squeezing her neck with his hands. She must have been terrified, unable to fight him off.

One woman went off in search of a Policeman, finding a Sergeant and two Constables in the Central Railway Station. The Sergeant and one Constable descended the steps, the other Officer barring public entry. The Officer`s pushed open each cubicle door in turn.. Joyce Liston was behind the only locked door, losing her life. The Officer`s made no further enquiries, and departed.

Wolens eventually emerged to wander the streets, probably spending the cash he had stolen from his victim. He turned up at Blyth Police Station just before midnight to report his heinous crime, but ignored. The body of Joyce Liston not yet discovered. The police offered Wolens a night in reception, "Where we can keep an eye on you," with a warning, "to be gone before 6 a.m. when early shift came on duty."

Wolens reported the murder to early shift. They ushered him out onto the streets with a suggestion, "go see your Probation Officer."
Wolens wandered the streets of Blyth until 9 a.m. when he spoke to his Probation Office and he made his report.

The murder of Joyce Liston was now filling morning news and the police called.

I represented Wolens at Newcastle Magistrates` Court and remanded to prison. He was a danger to the public and mentally disturbed. I obtained psychiatric reports and briefed my legal team.

Detective Inspector Arthur McKenzie met me at the lady`s toilet, Marlborough Crescent. An Officer stood guard as we descended the steps, a whiff of disinfectant in the air, mixed with urine. Pools of stagnant water and old torn magazines filled the cement floor. Fresco of male bodily parts depicting oversized penis`s and deformed genitalia adorned the walls along with vulgar jokes, some quite humorous and written in a variety of coloured lipsticks, mainly ruby red.

"Women can spell better than men" Arthur joked.

I stuck my head inside the cubicle. Such a small space, eerie and feeling abandoned, like a coffin.

The Crown Court Judge made an Order under the Mental Health Act. Wolens detained in a mental hospital for the rest of his life on the grounds of his diminished responsibility. No comment made about the night he spent on the reception bench of the Blyth Police Station.
I hung the indictment up the wall.

*

1988 I received a confidential letter from Marry MacMurray QC and one from Bill Hannah. Her Majesty the Queen had appointed them both Judges` of the Crown Court and I was delighted but our formidable legal team was over. I would instruct others.

They both deserved this great honour, reminded me of the occasion when I visited Mary at her home in Saltburn, to deliver a murder brief, one of many. Standing in the lounge, in a prominent position, was a magnificent grand piano.

"There is a story attached to that piano, Bert," Mary said, pouring two glasses of fine red wine.

"I was working in London at the time; for the Treasury, and decided to do a bit of shopping during my lunch. I had called into a shop in Oxford Street and was leaving when their security stopped me, suggesting I had items in my possession for which I had made no payment. Well you can imagine how I reacted, Bert. I found myself in the manager`s office where, in very short time, the matter was resolved…and to my satisfaction". She pointed to the piano. "I threatened to sue but the Chief Executive tendering his personal apologies offered me anything I wanted from the shop; for free.

"It is a nice piano isn't it"

Chapter Fourteen

"Brother on City Murder Charge," the headlines rang out.

Ronald Matthew Taylor, 22 years of age had stabbed his brother Leslie Taylor 32 years to death and it happened on Halloween, 31st October 1987.

Ronald and Leslie frequently argued, often coming to blows and on the evening in question, Leslie arrived at the Rockery Public House to fix disco lights for the party. Ronald went into town drinking, arriving at the pub about 9pm drunk and in a furious temper. They argued, threats made and and management asked Ronald to leave to prevent further disturbance. In the car park, Ronald lashed out at a parked car smashing two windows and dented the bonnet. He then made his way to his brother's home, barging inside and upsetting his young nephew and nieces and their babysitter, smashing the television set.

He then staggered home where he seized a knife saying, "I'm going to get him…"or "…I'm going to kill him."

The brothers met by chance on the corner of Springfield Road and Fairfield where Ronald drew his knife and, in a flash, stabbed his brother to death, the pathologist later confirming a wound to Leslie's chest 4 inches deep: chipping a rib before piercing his heart, liver and lung.

On arrest Ronald told police, "Les got hold of me by the neck. He tried to pull me to the ground. I grabbed the knife from the back of my trousers and stabbed him once. I intended to stab him, but not as seriously as I did, because he went down very quickly."

Ronald denied murder, admitting manslaughter but his pleas not acceptable to the Crown. We would have a trial to settle the issue. The jury at Newcastle Crown Court took only two hours to return a verdict of guilty of murder.

David Robson, QC prosecuting, told the court, "This was a sad case.

There had always been bad feeling between the brothers and they had often come to blows."

Jailing Taylor, Judge Angus Stroyan told him. "You fetched your brother into eternity with a single blow with a vicious and deadly knife. You had lost your temper on that night"

*

```
                          INDICTMENT                          No  ...452

The Crown Court at   NEWCASTLE UPON TYNE

THE QUEEN -v-    PAUL STOCKS and RONALD WILLIAM STOREY

              charged as follows:-

                         STATEMENT OF OFFENCE
         MURDER
                         PARTICULARS OF OFFENCE
         PAUL STOCKS and RONALD WILLIAM STOREY on a day between the 19th day of
         May 1988 and the 22nd day of May 1988 murdered Robert Emmott.
                              [signature]
                         OFFICER OF THE COURT

Form 5OLB
```

Paul Stocks and Ronald William Storey, were arrested for the murder of Robert Emmott. The incident happened on the night of the 23 May 1988 in a darkened back lane off Waterloo Street behind Rock Shots night club; a place frequented by homosexuals.

I arrived at the West End Police Station to represent both defendants but soon it became apparent there was a conflict. They were blaming each other for the murder and I could not represent both. As I had previously represented Storey, I telephoned Pearson and Caulfield, solicitors, inviting a representative to attend to look after the co accused, Stocks.

Both frequent visitors to Rock Shots they befriended Robert Emmott, a 23 years old barman following him into the back lane where the police would say they set out about Emmott, hitting him cruelly and violently with a concrete block, pulverising his face and head: blood spraying the brick wall and lying in pools.

The Officer in Charge of the investigation told me. "Unfortunately for these two, Emmott has a unique blood group and we have been able to link both men to the murder from blood samples collected in the bathroom of Stocks flat."

The officer continued: "We also have a witness who saw both men in Emmott's company earlier that evening." The witness saw Stocks follow Emmott into the back lane where he discovered dead.

"After the murder the defendant's walked to Stocks' flat in Waterloo Street, washed their bloody clothes in the sink and bath, then, we have information, they travelled to a restaurant in South Shields for a curry and a bottle of wine. We know all about their movements." The Officer studied his notes, "They came back to Newcastle, revisited the back lane to see if Emmott's body was still there… if he was dead."

"Forensics linked both men." He continued.

I visited the cell and spoke with Ronald Storey. He was calm and confident and denying everything except being in the back lane. He blamed Stocks but I was suspicious. I had previously represented Storey for violence but he was adamant he had nothing to do with Emmott's death.

"Stocks killed him" he told me, "I only tried to stop him. His blood may be on my shirt when I cuddled Emmott in my arms. I was shouting at Stocks to stop."

I relayed my instructions to my barrister and the forensic samples linking the two. There would be a trial.

During police interview, Storey's answers seemed well prepared, blaming Stocks for the whole incident and suggesting any blood on his clothing he could account for. Was he telling the truth or very cunning?

Stocks did not blame Storey.

They both spent several months on remand in prison whilst my legal team and I prepared for trial, visiting Storey in prison. We had to establish if Storey`s account was plausible. How his clothes` became contaminated? Did he embrace Emmott in the way suggested? Could our own forensic confirm his account as credible?

The trial lasted a week, the jury returning with their verdict: Stocks, guilty of murder. Storey acquitted. The jury had believed his account. My legal team had done their job, but I suspected the decision wrong.

Throughout the trial Stocks never blamed Storey, which was odd. He did not contest Storey`s evidence and he was given a life sentence.

I had to ask myself the question: Had they made a pact…an agreement? Stocks accept the murder, to let his lover walk free: the ultimate sacrifice.

I will never know the truth. That decision was for the jury, but the Prosecuting Barrister may have made an error. The police photographs served on the defence highlighted the indentation of a footprint stamped on Emmott`s chest, its size, its design, its style, even the amount of wear on the sole.

That shoe belonged to Storey.

*

I was in my office. I had an hour before my next appointment and I dusted and straightened my law books and the framed indictments. Kath dropped in with a cup of coffee as my thoughts drifted to my two years as trainee solicitor: when it all began.

"You will spend 6 months with Eric on crime," Mr Beecham the senior partner said, "then we will review your progress." My expert criminal knowledge and fourteen years as a detective would stand me in good stead. "Then you will spend time on family, house sales and purchases and personal injury." I would struggle with the others, but I knew I could bring clientele to the firm, and that was likely to sway them to keep me at the end of my Articles.

"Norman Peacock will give you instructions with regard to industrial tribunal work and family and you can sit with me when I see personal injury clients and civil disputes," he told me. "Peter Ross will show you how to buy and sell houses and do searches." I knew the law on each topic, but now needed to apply it to daily work.

The meeting at an end, Mr Beecham then drew me to one side: "I may also ask you to come out with me evenings to deliver flyers. Labour leaflets, in the Benwell area," his expression gave me the answer he wanted and I nodded, eagerly, although I always voted Tory. So I am a sycophant… sue me!

We got around to the subject of remuneration. How much they would pay for me working twenty- four hours a day, seven days week. They told me: I was worth £25 per week, plus travelling expenses and I managed a limp smile… from both my faces.

"Everything is geared for profit;" Jeremy said, departing.

I worried. How would I be able to support my wife and our two children on £25 per week? I was lucky to get this opportunity so I determined to grit my teeth and get on with it, hoping, in the not too distant future, to be a partner and share profits.

"Cover the police stations this weekend," Eric announced as I made my way up to the fourth floor.

"And if I have someone in custody" Norman piped up, "I will give you a call" Charming!

It was hard work and long hours, but the experience stood me in good stead when I made frequent contact with my former colleagues.

*

My first week and my call to attend a police station just happened to be Morpeth Police Station, a place I knew well. I would represent a teenage boy arrested on suspicion of a house burglary and I worried the kind of reception I would get from former colleagues. It could be a very embarrassing experience.

I rang the reception bell and waited. A detective rounded the door, a broad smile and pumping my hand. "You can make this an easy chalk (admission) for me, Bert" he said, leading me through to the custody suite. He and I had worked together in Ashington CID.

"You know your way" he said, shouting: "Bert's here lads. Get this man a coffee"

Five detectives herded round me like hungry wolves. "We've cracked it lads," one tec` shouted as the kettle screamed and coffee mugs rattled.

"Bert will get him to cough the job." He winked and I managed an embarrassing cough. They expected me to get my own client to admit his guilt, even if he is innocent.

A mug of steaming coffee pushed in my hand. "You like two sugars don't you Bert." Followed by small talk, "How's Anne and the kids?"

The conversation became personal. I had problems and only been in the station five minutes. I was uncomfortable but chatted, raising a smile when required, never forgetting I was on the other side of the law.

How I handled the situation would reflect my reputation for years to come and I let the conversation flow until we got down to business. Thankfully, I left with an innocent teenager and still on good terms with my former colleagues. I had done my job.

*

I headed for Newcastle Magistrates' Court, fighting my way up the main stairs, through the crowds, most on their way to the public gallery, eager to gloat and snigger at their pals expecting jail. Bets wagered, in cigarettes or drugs, on the length of each sentence, an entertaining day-out for idol minds.

I went into the remand court where I had two men in custody, both pleading for bail and I joined the queue of solicitors vying for poll position, sucking up to the court usher, coaxing him to let me on first.

I secured the freedom of one client, promising the other I would appeal to the judge of the Crown Court. "Maybe he will let you go home" I kept his hope up, then to Court 5, and a twenty year old charged with drugs. He was in the corridor leaning like the tower of Pizza, staggering like a crab towards me. I sweet hearted the lady- usher to call the case on next and he shuffled into the Dock standing facing the window. I hoped the Bench would not notice.

"Turn this way and pay attention," The court clerk demanded, and I turned and whispered, "look this way", as he swayed rhythmically. Time was short. I did not want the case stood down. I had a diary of appointments in the afternoon.

"What is your name?" the Clerk enquired. There was long silence, a swerve on his feet. The Clerk repeated: "What is your name, please?" looking at me as if I was responsible.

His head jerked, as if a bolt of lightning had struck his temple, then he clicked his fingers tunefully as saliva dribbled from his sloppy mouth and then he spoke: "Hey man, what name do you want? There`s a whole bunch of us up here."

The case over, he wandered out in a dream, none the worse or the wiser, he had been given a conditional discharge.

Court 3 and my client stood in the Dock charged with theft. He had a long list of offences and subject to a community order. The Chairman enquired: "Do you have children?"

"Yes" he replied.

"How old they are?"

My client loosened his trouser belt and pull up his shirt to expose his bare chest where the names and dates of birth of each child was tattooed upside down. He read each one to the Bench.

Drunk whilst driving, was the next case. The defendant held his driving licence in his hand ready to hand it over when disqualified The fact's read to the court. He was stopped whilst driving his Robin Reliant, three times over the legal limit The police officer's statement said: "The defendant was driving with one hand covering his right eye."

"Why?" I asked

"So I wouldn't see double."

My last case was an elderly woman: and a chronic alcoholic. She worried, and was right to worry she would be going to jail. "Ah was taw'ld last time I wuz in court ta' keep oot a trouble."

The Magistrate's listened to the facts, then announced: "You are very lucky. We are not going to send you to prison," she stopped shaking. "We will give you a fine" She rushed to the door, turned with a big smile, shouting to the Chairman, "Thanks pet, ah' hope ye get ya leg ower tonite"

*

A detective based at Throckley Police Station rang me. I will not divulge his name: "Come up," he said, "I have a prisoner in the cell confessing indecently assaulting a twelve year old girl."

I scribbled the details and headed for my car.

"An easy one for you Bert," he winked…don't forget I am selling my house and you will not be charging."

A long skinny student with a whiff of university sat hunched in the detention room his shoulders rounded. I introduced myself. We chatted: "I am told you indecently assaulted a young girl last Wednesday?" Tears rolled. He nodded.

I ran through the incident with him: "why did you do it?" I checked his antecedents. He had not been in trouble before. Then he broke down crying, tears cascading and protests of innocence. This was not the easy case: there would be no guilty plea.

"Why admit to it then?" I probed gently. "Why did you tell the officer you assaulted the girl if you did not?"

"He threatened to break my legs,"

I knew the detective and I knew how he worked He was a good cop, a good thief catcher but his enthusiasm sometimes got the better of him. He was a hulk of a man and with menacing eyes, reminded me of the film actor, Jack Palance.

I thought over the options. I would have to cross-examine the detective if we could not resolve the matter here and now.

"Do you have any witnesses" I probed, "an alibi, maybe, someone to say where you were on that day?"

He thought. "Yes I can," a eureka moment and he called out, "I was in London. I was staying at my girlfriend`s parent`s house.." Relief all over on his gaunt face: "So I could not have been in Newcastle… could I?"

I drove back to my office and phoned the detective. "Check his alibi."

He rang me back, "I have reviewed this matter. I have decided to release him. I have told him he could be prosecuted for making a false confession….but, what the hell, I have decided to let him go"

*

I went up to Kenton Bar Crown Court and sat behind my barrister waiting the appearance of the Judge. My Barrister read the pre- sentence report and passing time doodling. In a moment of joviality, he sketched on the back page, the contours of a buxom woman, her breasts large and exaggerated, adding the nipples then showing it for me to see. There was a call, "all stand" and the judge wandered in and the proceedings began. We bowed, regally, and my barrister smiling admiringly at his finished article.

"I don't have a copy of the pre-sentence report," the Judge announced, looking across the room at my barrister. "I see you have a copy," he waved a limp hand; "Let me have it please," directing the usher to comply with the task.

My barrister turning a delicious colour of puce, slipped the report into the usher`s hand, begging him to keep the back page low.

The judge reached for his spectacles, wrapping them round his ears then slowly he raised the report to eye level, studying the contents, page one…page two… then the sketch on the reverse.

"I will speak to you in my chambers," he pointed at my Barrister.

*

I took a walk to the Guildhall on the quayside, formally the Old Assizes and Merchants Court, overlooking the River Tyne and hidden under the High Level Bridge. Through the years, many a convicted prisoner has lost his life in that court.

I climbed the narrow stone steps to the first floor, the years peeling away with every step, back to the 19th century, the inside temperature dropping eerily with every step, into the long oblong hall and the dark oak surround, steeped in legal history. The ancient wooden Dock situated in the centre of the room, that final degradation ceremony for the doomed, the worn shackles and leg irons. That island few prisoner`s escaped.

His Lordship draped in red and heavily wigged, glaring down on the convicted prisoner with distain. I visualised him dragged in irons into the court, head shaved, shoulders rounded and bent in defeat as the sentence of the court announced his fate: the hangman`s noose.

The Jury room where the twelve good men deliberate, a paradox of visual confusion. The inner wall delineated in a masterful mural with rounded pillars and marble floor in herringbone design drifting off into the distance. No matter what position I took up, no matter where I stood, my eyes drawn mystically down the centre of the corridor to the bottom.

*

Saturday morning, wet and windy and our Northumbria Police Football Team are through to the semi-final of the league cup, a game we must win. Inspector John Wear, the team manager, determined to put out our strongest team, "We need every available player," he said, "they are a team with semi-professionals, but we can beat them."

Friday morning and I receive a call to attend North Shields Police Station. "Got one of your clients locked up for burglary," and soon I was speeding along the Coast Road and given the bad news, "He must remain in custody to appear in court tomorrow morning."

I flew back in my office and rang Inspector Wear. "Can`t play tomorrow John," I was almost in tears, "sorry but I have to attend Court."

There was a long silence.

"What you doing this afternoon?" He had a plan.

"In my office"

"Ring you back. Stay near the phone."

Within the hour, he called back. "Can you come to the Magistrates` Court for 3 pm? I have arranged a special Bench of magistrates."

"Magistrates do not sit on a Friday afternoon," I said.

"Get there. You will be free to play tomorrow."

The Magistrates` waited patiently: the defendant called into the Dock and in short time remanded to prison. "Hope you win" the Chairman said rising to leave the court. "Don't let this afternoon be for nothing"

We won three, one… we were through to the Final.

*

I was my own boss. I no longer answered to senior police officer`s breathing down my neck, demanding arrests, detections and promising to shape my career. I now held the reins to my future and I was happy: able take time off and fix holidays at my convenience.

Anne and I bought a new house, Kirksyde, a five bedroom detached house standing in an acre of gardens and situated in a quiet spot, three miles north of Pontelend, with panoramic views across the countryside. Our utopia: our dream home, although an unforeseen incident almost called the whole thing off. It was a sunny afternoon, in August, dry and hot when I decided to taken a cycle ride to look the house over. To admire the rolling lawns, the flower- bed's and the all-weather tennis court. We would have many hours on their.

I parked my bike at the gate side and peered over, picturing the change's I would make, then, out of the corner of my eye, I spotted the lady owner lying flat on her back, stark naked, sunbathing and only a few meters away. If she opened her eye's right then I could have been arrested as a peeping tom, a pervert and I panicked, jumping onto my bike and riding off like a bat out of hell, home. It took a strong moment to explain those events to Anne but gladdened by her response in hoots of laughter: "Wish I had been there to see it."

We spent many happy years at Kirksyde. Jane attended Church High, Jesmond where she gained excellent A levels, achieving her ambition to become an air-stewardess, flying Britannia Airways. Paul obtained a degree in law and qualified as a Barrister. We are so proud of them.

*

A call from my Eddie, brother: "I have arrested one of your clients. I will interview him at Newburn Police Station. He wants you to be present. Come up in half an hour."

I arrived within the hour and spoke to the custody sergeant: "No such prisoner here," he said, checking his computer. "Sure you were told he was at Newburn?"

Enquires then took me to Gateshead Police Station, where my client had been interviewed without me. My brother told him I was not available and the prisoner agreed to proceed without me. "What can I say? He's my brother.

"He changed his mind" Eddie told me, "and decided he did not want you." I suspected otherwise but the evidence was strong and he pleaded guilty: so no harm done.

Eddie later confessed to sending me on a wild goose chase, promising never to do it again.

*

I was at the Newcastle Magistrates` Court, hiding away in the solicitor`s private room, reading my files and waiting to be called inot court, when the door shot open and a solicitor, no names given, flew in, face flushed, and striding to the toilet. A Court Usher interrupted shouting "Your client wants to see you in Court Five." His response was hilarious: "Tell him to wait. I can only deal with one shite at a time"

Alan Finday, a solicitor and ex Northumbria Police Officer, was on his feet eloquently pleading for the release of his client when I slipped into the seat beside him. As the magistrates` withdrew to decide Alan whispered, "See that Magistrate sitting to the right of the Chairman?" He pointed to a pretty Magistrate, long blonde hair and a bright smile. I nodded, approvingly.

"Gonna` marry her," he gave a wink; but I knew he was already married.

When the Bench returned they remanded his client to prison and Alan shuffled off mumbling: "weddings off."

Chapter Fifteen

I was crunching numbers, checking my office piggy bank. Could I afford another car? My work took me to every court in Northumberland, often to Durham and mileage on my car was hitting 100,000 and rising. I trotted along to Fawdington, at Fenham Barracks to view a nice Mercedes Benz, a CL 500 and a reasonable price. I would think it over. Kath was waiting on my return, her coat over one arm and ready for home.

"An elderly couple would like to see you," she said, waving goodbye, "they don`t have an appointment but they seem a nice couple," he eyes pleading.

I would ring Fawdington later.

"Wheel them in then Kath" and an elderly couple, mid-sixties rounded the door, expressions of melancholy. I greeted them, offering a seat.

Mr Smith, I will call him, began to relay their story, his voice breaking; "Our son is dead," he dropped his head. That must have been hard to tell me. I waited. His hand reached for hers. She passed him her handkerchief.

"Our son was stabbed to death." He said, his shoulder`s lifting, his voice low. Silence followed then the story slowly unfolded: "Our son owned his own bungalow. He met a young woman. We liked her." she nodded her agreement.

"This girl moved in with our son, to live together, at his home. They loved each other. They seemed to be a happy couple, planning to marry. My son added her name to his house deeds to prove how much he loved her, but something, we do not know what, went wrong. She moved out and the wedding was off. She promised him she would see her solicitor, have her name removed from the title deeds."

"She promised she would do that." His wife confirmed.

"We think she did go to see her solicitor, but she did not go back to sign the deeds."

"Our son met another woman," his wife interrupted, "we didn`t like this one from the start but, it was not our place to interfere"

He continued: "After a short courtship she moved in to our son`s home." I wondered where this was leading me. His wife dabbed her eyes holding back the tears.

"We got a call from the Police, dreadful," he choked out the words, "she had stabbed our son… killed him."

I could not recall the incident, nothing in the newspapers or on television. I could not remember hearing the case passing through the courts.

"I know we cannot bring our son back," she said, "but we have lost our son and his home."

"His girl-fiend, the first one, never signed the house back to our son. She never took her name off the deeds and now she inherits the lot. She gets our son`s house…we get nothing."

I asked, "Will she transfer the house back to you as promised?" I told them I could inquire with Durham District Land Registry. See if the house held as Joint Tenants or Tenancy in Common.

I explained the difference in law. If his son and his girlfriend owned the house as Tenant`s in Common, then half the house moves to his parents. "It is something," I said

He dug into his pocket and produced a solicitor`s letter. It confirmed the girlfriend owned the house, absolutely, and she intended moving back in.

"Her own brother is angry with her" she spit out her words contemptuously. "He is on our side. He told her to give us back the house, but she has refused. Her brother and her parents have disowned her."

I apologised, "I am so sorry. There is nothing I can do"

They left heart broken.

My Mercedes had been sold. Life is shit.

Chapter Sixteen

October 1989, a call took me to Newburn Police Station. My next client, an active thief arrested on suspicion of handling stolen property.

Detective Larry Parish, an Irishman with over twenty year`s police service would question him. I knew Larry and his peculiar ways. Sometimes he was a better con artist than the conmen he arrested, and not always by the book.

Larry led me to the parade room. I sat at a large oblong wooden table, used to parade the next working shift and where the Sergeant would update his team regarding events occurring since their last shift and bring them up to date with criminal activity. I had sat at that desk on occasion.

I parked myself at the top of the table, throwing my brief case open, ready to make notes. The prisoner, my client, a man in his forties, deposited on to a seat to my right and Larry sat opposite him, leaning in close his elbows on the table, eyeball to eyeball.

The questions began in earnest, my client sitting back in silent disinterest, refusing to respond. He had been here many times before and knew the system. He would let Larry say his piece, but ignore him. I scribbled furiously.

Larry, as expected, was getting nowhere, giving the prisoner the evil eye and his well- rehearsed expression of disdain. "I`m gonna` have you mister," verbal hostility followed with my non- responsive client sitting casually in his seat. Larry`s broad Irish brogue became more aggressive, threatening him with unabated observation, 24 hours a day, psyching him out, staring at him in long silence: all part of Larry`s bag of tricks, then jumping up, leaning over and pointing an aggressive finger, promising he would, "spend the rest of his life in prison."

I scribbled every word then the interview suddenly stopped and I checked my watch: 36 minutes and Larry did not write down one word.

I closed my brief case and stood to leave.

"Did you get all that down, Bert?" Larry enquired. I nodded.

"Good" he smiled, "Send me a copy."

I knew Larry had a sense of humour, but he was serious so I posted him a copy. He telephoned, angry and hostile. "I have read your fucking note`s Bert. A pack of fucking lies, from start to finish" he growled, "so I`ve changed them. In my book he made full admissions and he will be charged."

I heard stifled laughter in the background. Larry was taking the piss.

The client had been released, NFA. (No further action)

*

Anne and I took our children off to Sunny Florida. Perfect age`s to meet Mickey and Donald and see the Walt Disney attractions. We drove to Manchester Airport, dropping our luggage off first then set off to find our prearranged car park, several miles south. We lost our way ending up driving west, the wrong way, on a dual carriageway and caught in a long stagnant queue of traffic several miles long. Time was running out.

Voices raised, tempers frayed. We were at serious risk of missing our flight.

A few choice words passed Anne`s lips, including an order to: "Do something," so I jumped out and ran to the car in front, begging directions to our destination, then slipping along the emergency lane, and twisting and turning through back streets. More by good luck then judgement, we arrived at the multi storey park with minutes to spare; several families destined for the same flight waiting impatiently, the engine of the bus ticking over, ready to leave. We scrambled on board, composing ourselves and made our flight with only minutes to spare.

Eight hours later and bleary- eyed, resetting our watches to local time, we landed at Bangor Maine.

It was two in the morning when we cleared Custom`s and herded back onto our flight for another one and a half hours flight, passing New York on route to Orlando International Airport where the sultry tones of Walter Cronkite echoed across the loud speaker.

Temperature in the 70's, the sky coral blue, this ex copper was more excited than the kids as we drove in our hire car to Holiday Inn on International Drive.

I kicked off my shoes. They were tight and I had a problem. My left ankle had swollen to three sizes bigger than my right. I suspected Deep Vein Thrombosis, but it was not going to spoil our holiday.

We spent the fortnight living on burgers, coke, French fries, apple pie with buckets of ice cream. Visiting attraction double-time, Sea World, Epcot, Disney Land, Wet and Wild, Kennedy Space Centre then a long flight home, jet-lagged and a crushing pain in my left leg.

DVT confirmed, I was lying in a private bed at the Nuffield hospital, Jesmond, within the hour hooked up to a line of Heparin, warfarin and daily blood tests.

"You are lucky to be alive," the consultant remonstrated: "If a piece had broken off and travelled to your heart you would be lying in a coffin, not this bed"

*

Ten days later, I escaped the Nuffield, slipping back to work, spending most of my time at Police Headquarters, giving legal advice to police officer's facing allegations of unlawful arrest, criminal damage or excessive use of force, solving domestic disputes and matrimonial issues. An interview by a senior ranking officer attached to Complaints & Discipline (now Professional Standards) often lasted more than four hours some in excess of six hours, then followed a further two hours of breeches of force discipline

Interviews were hand written, now replaced with tape recordings where every word recorded. Should one Officer have to attend court to answer criminal charges, I would represent him and am proud to say I was able to defend every one successfully, maintaining the high reputation of Northumbria Police.

*

My work for the Police Federation gained regular invitations to the Senior Officer's Dinning-In, at HQ where penguin suit and bow ties` were compulsory and speeches` rebounding off visiting dignitaries both jovial and fraternal. One speech saw me as victim when the Superintendent told the congregation: "I am pleased to see Bert Gibson, our Federation Solicitor, is present. He successfully defended one of our officers` allegedly smoking in bed and setting fire to his blanket," there was a short pause: "Bert won the case" he smiled over at me: "He proved the blankets were already on fire before the officer got in." Laughter filled the room.

Chapter Seventeen

A balmy evening, the smell of country air, calves and lambs wandering passed our garden, dancing and playing in the fields. A perfect day for trimming hedges and cutting lawns, then an urgent call from Police HQ A client had shot a woman and wanted for attempted murder. They had surrounded a house in Sunderland but he was refusing to come out and he held a young girl hostage. They hoped I could sway him to come out without anyone being hurt. He still had the gun.

I was at Police HQ in minutes. A patrol car waiting: blue light`s flashing, engine revving and ready to take flight. I had time to click my seat belt into place and we were off, screaming through Ponteland village, parting traffic and touching 70 mph passed St Mary`s Church, sweeping across the River Pont, manoeuvring between startled drivers and only inches to spare.

My stomach would catch up.

The Metro Centre loomed in minutes, siren blasting a warning, holding centre ground and flying, mac 11, to Washington Services where another patrol car awaited.

"I don't know Sunderland area" my driver apologised, "I`m traffic North. We will follow that car into Sunderland,"

We tucked in behind, flashing through Washington when a broadcast echoed over the car radio: "stand down. One man arrested. No casualties," That was music to my ears. I did not cherish the prospect of talking to someone holding a gun.

We arrived at the Police Station at a much more leisurely pace.

He was in the cell now minus the gun, an athletic 6 footer with muscles and a tense expression of impatience:

"The gun went off by accident, Bert," he protested. "It was an accident, I promise. I didn`t mean to shoot her." He raised a hand, shoulder height, forming a fictitious gun with his index finger pointing at my face. Very close. "Look this is what happened," demonstrating. I was intimidated standing there under the protection of several officers. He pulled the trigger and I could almost hear the bang.

"See, Bert. Look at my finger. It`s deformed," there was a noticeable bump at the joint but if that was his defence he was in serious trouble. For obvious reasons now was not the time to tell him.

He relayed the events: Owed a debt, today was pay back, and he wanted his money plus interest His reputation in the underworld depended on it.

He drove to a house in Houghton Lee Spring, parking in the back lane and calling the occupant on his mobile. He could not get in. The metal gates padlocked. He expected the debtor to appear but a woman opened the yard door and looked out. She turned but the gun blasted a hole in her back and she fell, blood oozing. She crawled inside and called an ambulance.

I represented him at Sunderland Magistrates` Court. A battalion of armed police secured the corridors and he remanded to prison; his history of violence well documented.

At Durham Crown Court, he pleaded guilty and received a sentence keeping him in prison long after I retire.

*

A detective based at Forest Hall Police Station rang me at home. He had arrested a suspect for unlawful wounding. He asked me to attend. "He has asked for you, Bert"

I hadn`t know this man. Odd I thought but agreed to attend. I suspected something was wrong. This detective did not ring solicitors unless there was an angle, something he would not disclose to me. I did not trust him.

The prisoner was in the cell, calm and relaxed. Too relaxed for my liking, his leg's spread comfortably across the wooden bench, a pillow under his head. This police station did not give prisoner's pillows. It was like a hotel. He was not suffering the usual anxieties associated by suspect's about to be interviewed for a serious assault and a lengthy prison sentence at the other end.

We talked. He chatted, denying the allegation, but it was as if he was reading a script and I suspected he knew the result of his interview and the outcome: too confident, too cocky.

The interview began. It was as if the suspect anticipated each question, as if he knew what was coming next, giving slick answers and performing like a professional criminal, denying everything.

Then I caught the detective smiling at the prisoner. A smile that said, `you're doing well, keep it up`. The interview ended in minutes and without the usual deep probing questions or aggression. No effort to trip him up or call him a liar and the suspect was ushered out of the police station before I gathered my papers. There would be no criminal charges today.

Later I learned the prisoner was the detective's informant; his grass, and a direct link to detecting crimes and criminal activity. The detective had used me to legitimize the interview and protect his informant.

Chapter Eighteen

"Detective Inspector McKenzie is on the phone," Kath said, "He would like a word." Arthur a long –time friend and the giant of a man lifted heavy weights most of us would leave to cranes: his arms like Popeye`s, biceps as big a tree trunks. He tamed the villains on notorious Scotswood Road, all by himself.

"Bert" his voice courteous and gentle: "I have a job for you."

When Arthur rang, it was best to listen. "A man is going to step off the train at Newcastle Central Station at five O`clock. I have told him to call into your office." My brow lifted. What did he have planned for me? Arthur lived on the edge.

"10 years ago this fella escaped from Liverpool prison. He`s been on the run ever since, now wants to give himself up."

"Not your simple theft from shop then Arthur?" I quipped.

"Put him in your car and bring him up to Newburn Police Station. I am on a day off but will be wandering the corridors when you arrive."

Only Arthur could get involved in something like this, but at 5 p.m., there was a knock on my office door and a man walked in, bag over his shoulder, an expression of defeat. We did not say one word and I deposited him into Arthur`s custody and never saw the man again.

*

Autumn1986. Detective Inspector John Rosebrough, Regional Crime Squad, wandered in parking himself on the edge of my desk. "I am travelling down to the midlands, Bert, and you are my cover.

Where I will be, what I will be doing, you don't need to know," he wrote down a telephone number, pushing it under my nose. "I will be meeting some bad people, and if things go wrong, they may ring you" he dropped the note onto my desk. "Just tell them you're looking to buy property."

John and I have been friends for years, socials and playing football. We worked the Minnie Beck murder at North Shields. She was the Landlady of a pub on the quayside and foreign sailors, their ship moored nearby, suspected.

Minnie had been bludgeoned to death and several bags of silver three-penny pieces stolen. By the time we had set up the incident room at North Shields Police Station, the ship had already left for Southampton. Detective Inspector Jim Stephenson OIC sent three detectives south to question those on board, but we suspected the evidence thrown overboard. Sadly, the murder remains undetected.

John got up to walk out. I had feelings of vulnerability. I was no longer a copper, no longer a member of the biggest gang in the country. I did not have the protection of a Police Warrant Card and, if these bad asses discovered the truth, they might pay me a visit. I decided not tell Anne.

*

Monday morning the last week of November, a quiet weekend lay ahead.

Ray Mitchell, Chairman of the Northumbria Police Federation, rang, "Can you come to Force HQ?" "A disciplinary hearing has been arranged for 3pm this afternoon involving a sergeant and two constables and they will appear before the Chief Constable: they may be sacked.

I met my client, the constable most involved in the alleged conspiracy and a seasoned copper with eight years in the job. Geoff Forester, solicitor, and my football colleague, would represent the sergeant and the other constable.

He relayed the incident.

Working nightshift alone, patrolling the bottom end of Gateshead High Street, checking doors and windows and seeing drunks off the streets, the usual things, when he received a call of "intruders on the premises" at a nearby petrol station. It was going midnight when he arrived on foot, a dim light casting shadows inside the kiosk, glass from the door scattered on the ground.

"I cupped my hands and peered through the glass," he said, "something moved. I heard a muffled noise and decided to climb inside"

He had no backup. I thought him very brave. "I didn`t know who or what might be inside." Dropping to his knee`s he climbed through the broken window. "It was dark" he said, "who- ever was inside was behind the shelves." I made notes.

"A street lamp cast a shadow onto the inner wall. A display stand blocked my view. I drew my truncheon and called out, "POLICE: COME OUT, moving slowly to the rear; truncheon raised. Someone was inside". He said, "THIS IS THE POLICE. COME OUT, NOW."

"I was shitting myself," he half smiled. "I did not know who was inside; possibly a drunk or a druggy, maybe mentally disturbed: maybe with a weapon."

"Something moved and I leapt on it, grabbing hold tight. He was a big bugger; as big as me," he said, "He resisted and we fought, tumbling to the floor, shelves and stock flying and I brought my truncheon down hard….more than once."

"I couldn`t let him get the better of me, not in there. In that confined space. I did not know if he had anything on him, something he could use on me. I pinned him hard with my truncheon… "

Blood splattered everywhere, he said, on the walls, my uniform, on the floor but he was my prisoner." the officer relived every second. "I might have hit him too many times?" He confessed, "But, I was alone in a confined space."

His Sergeant and a Probationer Constable soon arrived to offer assistance and bring the prisoner outside, then off to hospital. "He had several head wounds, needing stitches."

They then returned to the garage. They wanted to look at the CCTV camera situated across the other side of the road. It may have recorded the incident. My client worried it may have shown him using too much force. They went to the security office and asking to view the incident.

Two civilian Security Officers were in charge of the cameras. They refused so the Sergeant seized it as evidence and they watched it in the parade room.

"No wonder they didn`t want anyone to see it," he blushed. "The security men spent hours watching drunken young couples having rampant sex on the grass, against a wall, even over the bonnet of a car, and in positions that could have scored high marks at the Olympic Games."

"My arrest was also on view. It showed me climbing inside and hitting the burglar. Even when he was subdued and no longer a threat"

His Sergeant made an executive decision to destroy the evidence, not realising there was a hard copy still in the security office which the prosecuting barrister would present during the hearing.

I had to mitigate the circumstances, to lessen the harm to my officer, achieve the best result possible.

"The officer was brave," I said. The Chief Constable agreed.

"He went into a dark, confined space, not knowing who or what he would face or if there was a weapon." The Chief agreed.

I conceded the destruction of the video was wrong… but reminded him the burglar had made no complaint.

"The burglar has fully recovered"

The Sergeant reduced in rank. My client to forfeit one year`s increase in salary and the probationer constable given a verbal warning.

*

I headed south to Peterlee Police Station. My client detained for an alleged deception.

I met the detective investigating: "He told an elderly man he was a builder and he needed his roof repaired. He charged him thousands of pounds but he didn`t do the work,"

The elderly man was then frog marched to the bank to draw out the money, "But we were waiting for him."

I went into the cell. He had a history of conning elderly people this way. He denied everything. "I had nothing to do with it. It wasn't me." I expected this reply.

Identification would to be an issue. I told the detective and an identification parade, a line up, arranged. Could the elderly man recognise him?

Nine men of similar description were in the line. My client could occupy anywhere in the line he wanted.

"Don't make eye contact," I said, "That will draw his attention to you. Look straight ahead and fix your eyes on the far wall…and most of all, do not speak to him." I insisted.

He joined the line. The elderly man entered the room.

"Take your time…be sure before you say anything…" The Inspector encouraged, "just point to the man you recognise, if he is here."

He walked slowly along the line, pausing, looking closely at each one, particularly the man occupying position five. My client stared back at him, watching his every move, forgetting my instructions.

"That's him," he pointed at my client and then the suspect sealed his own fate.

"Are you sure?" he asked.

"Yes I am sure?" I shook my head in disbelief. The Inspector scribbled down every word said, handing the notes to me to sign as a witness.

"Your client has been very helpful."

He would spend a few more Christmases in jail.

*

Consett Magistrates' Court and three men detained in custody, accused of robbery. I represented one, John Foley also a criminal law specialist, represented the other two. We made applications for their bail but sent to

Durham prison.

John and I attended a Judge in his private Chambers at Durham Crown Court. His Honour Judge Bill Hannah, formerly part of my murder team granted bail to two: one my client, the third defendant would remain in custody.

We returned to Consett Magistrates' Court for committal proceedings, the same Chairwoman on the Bench. She took exception to the two men now on bail: "what are they doing out of jail? I remanded them all into custody," and promptly sent them back to prison.

Our protestations were overruled and we hotfooted back to see Judge Hannah, who expressed annoyance that a lower court had overruled the decision of a Judge and once again he released them. "Heads will roll, for over ruling a more senior court," he insisted.

"You must proceed to the High Court. The Chairman has no power to do such a thing."

Their Lordships' at the High Court in London refused to hear our application, deciding wheels would roll behind the scene. The Chairwoman never sat again in Consett Magistrates' Court.

*

Friday evening and I was at Consett Police Station. My client detained for court the following morning. I was playing football: far more important so I could not attend personally. Stephen, my partner attended, tasking instructions and promising to ask for bail.

9:30am and Stephen made his way to the Magistrates' Court to find the main doors locked He peered inside and wrapped on the glass, hoping to catch some ones attention, then knocked several times and calling out. After much time lost, security let Stephen inside and he rushed into Court to find his client had already stood before the court, unrepresented, and remanded to Durham prison.

Stephen was furious, explained his predicament. "That is unfair," he protested. "The Court doors were locked. I could not get in… the police knew I was attending this hearing."

The Bench refused to hear him, "This Court cannot wait for solicitors who arrive late."

Monday morning and appraised of the injustice, I headed for Durham Crown Court and to the Judge's private Chambers, to express my annoyance at the injustice.

"He has a right, in law, to be represented" I protested, "to make an application for bail. The magistrates' were wrong to refuse him that right," I laid it on thick, lodging my strongest protest.

The Judge looked casual, unresponsive.

"What do you want?" he asked uncaringly.

"I seek justice, Your Honour, for my client," I got a short reply.

"NO."

Ushered outside, I realised that justice was not for everyone and all the beating of my chest and pleas for fairness, could be for nothing: a sober lesson.

I could only do my best, then let the dice fall. To worry otherwise would put me into an early grave.

*

December 1989 I moved to new office's in Mosley Street, renting seven large rooms on the second floor. I excluded the clause in the lease to repair/replace the rackety old lift when it finally fell to pieces. Its use was to risk life and limb, teeth jarring as it took off, the old fashioned concertina gate opening and closing with a loud squeal.

Kath and Carol Gibson (no relation to me), her daughter Louise, Paula, Kath Smith, Sheena Rumbold and Nicola Dodd were my new crew. Anne would continue accounts and the wages; we were a happy team.

Mid-afternoon 2nd December, I will remember as one of the most harrowing cases of my career.

A respectable, decent, single young woman, no name given, was arrested for murdering one of her baby son`s and the attempted murder of the other: a harrowing and distressing case for which, Kath, my secretary who would have to type out the trauma of the whole incident.

Questions echoed around my office: Why would a loving, caring mother do such a thing, murder her child?

Medical experts, far more intellectual than me would decide.

The story unfolded. She had placed her babies on her bed and then lay beside them. I cannot begin to understand what trauma she was going through or what was in her troubled mind but, what I can only describe as madness took place when she reached for a pillow and placed it over her child`s face, suffocating it. She then turned to the other child, pressing the pillow down onto its face but, whether she came to her senses or heard the child`s cries, I don`t know, but she withdrew the pillow and the second child lived.

A Policewoman sat outside the open cell door, suicide watch. The inner cell light subdued. I offered my heart-felt sympathy. I have two children of my own. She was hysterical, curled-up in the corner, frightened, distressed and confused, unable give me an explanation.

Medical experts and eminent psychiatrists from St Nicholas Hospital would submit their reports.

David Robson QC and I attended the secure unit to find her much improved, but with a long way to go. We were unable to broach the subject of her detention. "Too painful"

Medical reports formed the entire defence.

We would raise the defence of Infanticide, a legal defence available in such harrowing cases where a mother kills her child within twelve months of giving birth, the death caused by an illness known as lactation; a form of mental depression.

At the Newcastle Crown Court, she received much sympathy and understanding and an order to detain her for medical treatment. We hoped she would soon be well and reunited with her child.

*

George Stainsby, a sole practitioner, occupied the first floor of the building with his wife Elizabeth. George and I decided to merge our two firms.

My daughter, Jane left Church High school with good `A` levels and decided she wanted to be an Air Stewardess, flying around the world. She needed experience dealing with the public so I took her in as my Crown Court Clerk. She attended trial`s and conference`s and recorded judgements. She worked well and many new clients, particularly young men, walked through my door for representation…but I soon realised they were hoping to see Jane.

During prison visits, Jane accompanied me. I would ask questions of the prisoner but they replied to Jane. She joined Britannia Airways, flying across the world, and Anne and I often stood at the departure lounge waiving her off…and a safe journey.

Paul left university with a 2/1 degree, securing pupillage in Durham Barristers` Chambers. He gained a tenancy in Durham then moved to Cathedral Chambers, Queen`s Street, Newcastle where I was able to provide him with a variety of criminal cases, including the murder trial of Graeme Duncan. Paul settled for a position as a Senior Crown Prosecutor, doing his utmost to put my clients in jail.

Chapter Nineteen

Alan Swindon was wanted for murder.

On the night of 10th November, he fatally stabbed Paul Furness and then attempted to murder Neil Cowen. The Police are anxious to trace him and, Crime UK, broadcast the urgency across the screen. Swindon, 26 years of age, of Elliott Drive, Felling, Gateshead, spends his evenings and weekends drinking in local pub's and night clubs and known to carry a knife.

Swindon was drinking heavily in Walkers nightclub, Low Friar Street, Newcastle and near closing time he demanded more alcohol. The young barmaid politely refused, "it's after drinking hours."

Swindon was angry. In front of his friend's she had embarrassed him. She had shown him disrespect and you do not do that to Alan Swindon.

He slapped her hard across her face, knocking her off her feet then wrapped a telephone cord around her neck. She was terrified, crying, but she was lucky, he did not use his knife, instead wandering out into Low Friar Street, joining the gathering, celebrating crowds.

"Swindon was out of control," John Milford QC would tell the Crown Court.

"He was looking for trouble and he approached Paul Furness, a total stranger, celebrating his recent engagement. For no reason, he picked a fight with Paul Furness, plunging the knife deep into his chest and then turned to Neil Cowen, stabbing him," Milford told the jury.

Swindon hailed a taxi and headed south across the Tyne. He attended a party and then he went to ground. For several weeks, the manhunt was on, with extensive police enquiries and televised broadcasts. "We want to speak to Swindon urgently."

"Do you know where he is?" the Superintendent asked me.

"Sorry. I have no idea." Police records confirmed I represented Swindon.

Crime Watch UK flashed Swindon's photo across the screen. "This man is dangerous. Do not approach him."

Alan's mother rang me. The police asked her to go on television: to ask her son to give himself up. Mrs Swindon asked me to accompany her. She feared the police might shoot him.

"I know he has not been a good lad, but I don't want him to die."

The broadcast would be at Gateshead Police Station, first floor. The cameras were waiting. I grabbed my coat, hurried down my office steps and carelessly stumbled, tearing the sole off my shoe. It hung open like a big tongue, but I did not have time to change as time was pressing, the glare of the light's awaited. I limped into the Police Station and met Mrs Swindon, shuffling along the corridor, my sole flopping noisily on the floor tiles.

The camera's rolled.

"Eee… hey…Alan, son… give ya sell up. For God's sake lad… let is na where ye are."

Alan arrested weeks later on a tip off from the public, and without incident or in jury.

At Leeds Crown Court, Swindon denied murder.

The trial lasted two and a half weeks.

Swindon admitted stabbing Furness in the thigh, but he blamed Furness for "walking onto my knife." He admitted assaulting the barmaid but denied stabbing Neil Cowen.

The jury deliberated for nine hours returning with a guilty verdict on each count. He received a twenty four year's jail sentence, including eighteen months for assaulting the barmaid.

Time had past between the murder and Swindon's arrest, but the Furness family had suffered unnecessarily. H.M. Coroner could not release their son's body for burial until I had obtained a post-mortem. I could not instruct a pathologist until I had the benefit of legal aid authorising the expense.

I rang the Clerk to Newcastle Magistrates' Court asking for a legal aid certificate. He politely refused, "not until Swindon is arrested. He must personally sign the forms." The body of Paul Furness would remain at the mortuary. I could do nothing to help his family.

The position was unacceptable.

I sent a letter to the Home Office. I asked them to look at the situation, urgently. I asked them to intervene and grant the legal aid certificate, for the sake of the Furness family and other families faced with a similar tragic situation.

My letter was ignored.

*

Tartan rockers: The Bay City Rollers said "Bye Bye Baby" to £5000 worth of their musical equipment. It was the night of 19th December 1991, when David Gates decided to steal their Transit van.

The 1970's one time chart-toppers had played in front of a near capacity crowd at the Gateshead Leisure Centre and were to perform the following night at the Temple Park Leisure Centre, South Shields, when drunken David Gates decided to deprive them of their equipment.

Following his arrest, I spoke to the more sober 21 year old. He told me he just wanted to, "save the world from the sound of the Bay City Rollers."

A repentant, David Gates, appeared before Gateshead Magistrates' Court charged with stealing guitars, cymbals and lighting equipment. He pleaded guilty, disqualified from driving and sentenced to a community service order.

*

"One of Britain's Biggest Forgery Rings," was the headlines in the local press. Four men arrested in connection with a multi-million dollar forgery, instigated by Cheviot Printing, a small printing firm, based in

New Bridge Street, Newcastle. They had spent month`s churning out millions of forged $20 notes.

The hearing would take place in Preston Crown Court where Prosecuting Barrister, Brian Levinson, told the High Court Judge: "The type of paper used to perfect the forged Bills was exactly the same as that used by the U.S. Mint."

The prosecutor presented several Bills as exhibits: "The defendants managed to duplicate the complicated double colour printing process,"

Cheviot Printers initial intention was to make dollar notes as a gimmick, with a cartoon character circled in the centre but realised they had the expertise to perfect the dollar bill: "and turned out millions, until a member of staff informed the police."

Four men, including my client John Appleby, were behind the conspiracy, but it took the North East Regional Crime Squad a further nine months to gather evidence and complete their investigations.

John Appleby, a native of Alnwick, told the police: "No way can I tell you anything. I would get my knee caps blown off."

Before Preston Crown Court stood the defendant`s: Barry Armstrong, 34, of St.Buryan Crescent, Newcastle, John Appleby, 33, the Crown Inn, Alnwick, Malcolm Logan, 36, Springhill Gardens, Benwell, Newcastle and Peter Stephenson, 37, The Headlands, Darlington, each to be represented by separate Counsel.

Mr Justice Caulfield presiding.

The defendant`s pleaded not guilty. There would be a trial, and a date fixed several weeks hence.

His Lordship was to consider bail or custody pending the trial date. He decided to allow them bail with one condition: to reside at their home address, but what happened next was so humorous that the incident could have been on television

His Lordship first dealt with Appleby: "Stand up,"

Appleby jumped to his feet, head bowed.

"You shall reside at Alllnnnwwwiiiccckkkk, mispronouncing the town of Alnwick.

Bill Hannah, my barrister, promptly rose to his feet to correct His Lordship pointing out his error. Not one prone to make errors, His Lordship seemed offended by such impertinence, well intentioned or not and insisted thereafter he confirm the correct pronunciation of every defendant's address, and to Counsel's embarrassment. My barrister was up and down like a yoyo with tittering around the court.

The morning of the trial arrived. Police Officers would to give evidence. The judge would not countenance delay. He would be in London by the end of the week.

His Lordship entered the Court in regal fashion: horse- hair wig resting on his narrow shoulders his red robe giving the occasion eminence.

His Lordship needed an indictment, confirming the charge against each defendant, demanding of the prosecuting barrister: "Where is my Indictment?"

"My Lord" he rose, trembled: "I am distressed,"

"Don't be distressed…" the Judge, replied, abruptly, "… just give me an Indictment."

The jury quickly sworn in, His Lordship calling the police witnesses to give their evidence at double speed, His Lordship turning to the jury and smiling, sardonically, to get them on his side, then berating any defence barrister having the temerity to ask even one question of the officers..

"What could you possibly want to ask this officer?" he scowled over powering the defence barristers into humbled submission, or risk the wrath of his Lordship. Is Lordship ruled the Court and everyone in it with an iron fist.

Time, not justice was of the essence.

The trial, listed for four days, was over in two days, the Jury swayed by His Lordship's to convict.

On the afternoon of the second day of trial, His Lordship decided the sentence: "Stand up," He demanded, "You will all go to jail for three

years." It was over.
 We decided we had no grounds to appeal.

Chapter Twenty

Our Government decided lawyers were spending too much money on legal Aid. The Lord Chancellor cryptically remarking he would, "squeeze the legal profession until it squealed." reminding me of the Shakespeare play: Henry V1; "First let`s kill all the lawyers."

Although payment for legal aid has not raised for many years our illustrious Government, set a course that would ensure the closure of many solicitors` offices throughout England and Wales with consequential staff redundancies. Young Law graduates, intent on joining the profession, would not find employment.

"Lawyers are making millions," the press falsely reported, when in truth the typical high street practice barely survives, working eight months a year paying wages and office overheads before earning a penny in profit.

Our newspapers made good reading but the smell of falsehood still lingers in the public domain.

The system of payments of legal aid changed. No longer reflecting actual hours worked preparing, researching and attending court. Standard Fees ruled. A set fee paid for representing guilty pleas, a higher fee for trial`s, neither one reflecting the true value of work undertaken in each case, visiting clients in prison, tracing witnesses, obtaining expert forensic and medical reports.

"Franchising will whip you into shape," the Government announced, imposing obligatory visits to our offices and demanding examination of confidential client files and carrying out a detailed paper chase. A five-year`s business plan was introduced, but our legal aid franchise contract only lasted two years. A pile of forms to fill in each day: costly high tec` computers installed.

The changes had their desired effect as High Street firms closed their doors, some venturing into partnerships, mergers and amalgamations but with little foresight how it could work in practice.   I am reminded of the Beecham days and closing our railways.

Diversify or die our government preached, while they allowed public funds to haemorrhage in search of untenable ventures such as the Millennium Dome and M.P`s expenses and taking our young soldiers into an illegal war. Big brother held the whip hand and struck deep wounds across the back of the legal profession.

"Get involved in politics or be governed by your inferiors," A quote from a man much wiser than me and, with the stroke of the pen, we lawyers became legal sales reps, vying for our next client, and begging for our monthly legal aid cheque simply to survive.

Long- standing professional ethics between lawyers now cast aside and replaced with dishonour in the pursuit of the next client.

A courteous and gentle way of life, which has stood the test of time, replaced with the stigma of touting and advertising for business on television (ambulance chasers) and unsolicited circulars pushed through doors.

It is almost war on the high street between lawyers as camaraderie replaced by verbal disagreement, denigrating the high esteem of our profession: Backs against the wall and the survival of the fittest.

When I qualified as a solicitor not too many years ago, and during my service as a Police Officer, the lawyer considered a dignified step up, honest and reliable. "My word is my bond," and the unwritten rule held sway that a client remained with his solicitor his entire life and with no desire for change.

Rarely, confronted with a client seeking to transfer from one firm to another but, no matter how rare, we, individually and collectively, would do the honourable thing and seek to resolve the issues by sending the client back to his own solicitor. " I hope you can resolve your differences" Only after much consideration would a solicitor take on the new case from another firm, as integrity and respect for one`s colleague reigned paramount.

Today, I am saddened to say, the new generation of lawyers are inclined to abuse and demean each other. I have witnessed lawyers offering bribes to clients, engaging in underhand tactic`s to sway them to his firm and throwing into the gutter those bastions of integrity and dignity.

We now treat the criminal client like a precious diamond elevating them above their place in society. Solicitor`s offer him a choice. "Do you want him or me?" and lowering the reputation of the lawyer to his level. Defendant`s referring to their solicitor by first name, as if they are long standing buddies: on equal terms. I laughed at one of our new generation of lawyers who successfully defended his client on no less than six occasions, winning each criminal trial in succession and keeping him from jail, to find the client now represented by another solicitor.

"Why have you dropped me when I have achieved so much success for you?"

"You have been great. You are a good lawyer. I was happy with you, but your luck was bound to run out sometime, and I don't want to go to jail"

Chapter Twenty One

Late evening of 6th March 1992, "Come down to Sunderland Police Station. We have locked up Thomas Wilson Mitchell for murder," was the call from Superintendent Goff Nicholson.

Within the hour I was at the Sunderland Police Station and briefed about a man I can only describe as being the most vile, perverted man, I would ever represent.

I listened as Superintendent Nicholson briefed his team of detectives. The evidence was overwhelming. There would not be a trail. Thomas Wilson Mitchell had already made his admission and would be pleading guilty and from the circumstances outlined, I would need psychiatric reports.

"The worst murder I have ever investigated," one detective whispered, "I don't envy you this one."

I flicked through an album of photographs of the victim and my stomach churned. For many years, I had attended post mortems and witnessed bodies` dissected by the pathologist, but I wasn`t prepared for what I was shown.

I took a walk along the corridor to Mitchell`s cell. He was sitting on the edge of the wooden bench, his personal belonging, shoe- lace`s, his leather- belt, lying on the floor outside where a policeman kept observation. Our public would have no sympathy for this man. They would want him sent to prison for a very long time. Only then would the thirst for revenge be satisfied.

"Revenge is a dish best served cold."

Mitchell, 31 years of age, glanced my way. I dropped my brief case at my feet and introduced myself. He was distant, subdued, trembling. His head on his chest and wringing out his hand`s as if still covered in blood I took an instant dislike to Thomas Wilson Mitchell but determined he would get a fair hearing and my legal team would ensure his plea was the right one.

He spoke, timidly, about what he had done, probably easing his guilt. He had already purged his conscience in his confession to the police.

The horror of the incident unfolded: He had left his home wearing his wife's underwear and carrying a chisel and plastic ties tucked into his pocket. "I didn't mean to hurt" he sobbed, but when he knocked on his victim's door he intended raping her. The neighbour he told me he liked. He did not mean her harm.

I noted his brief instructions: That morning his wife had left for work. He slipped into her underwear and watched pornographic videos. He had the obsession to rape a woman, any woman he told me, particularly Carol Timm who lived with her husband across the street.

He emptied his troubled mind into my note pad, my thoughts drifting back to the 1960's and time I spent at the Criminal Investigation Training College, Wakefield where a Home Office pathologist presented photographs of body parts. Innocent human beings fatally injured and who suffered appalling wounds.

"Murder" he told his audience: "is usually committed in the most harrowing, traumatic way. He will have difficulty coming to terms with what he has done. He may even convince himself it was someone else. You have to get to him, quickly, and stop him before he does it again."

Mitchell lived with Maureen his wife, in Sulgrave Village, Washington. They lived opposite Paul and Carol Timm, "a nice friendly couple," he said.

Outwardly, Mitchell was jovial and a good neighbour, chatting whenever they met.

Paul Timm's had suffered stomach cancer and Carol had been there throughout, supporting and helping him recover. They were a devoted couple.

The press would report Carol as, 'a lovely lady'.

Unknown to the Timm family and hidden from his wife, was the psychopathic mind of a killer and the moment to act out his perverted fantasy had arrived.

Mitchell waited until his wife left for work, pretending he was too poorly and needed to stay at home. He then rummaged through his wife's underclothes, pulling on her basque, her camisole, her fishnet stockings, dancing around the room watching pornographic videos.

He wanted sex. Vile, brutal, perverted sex and Carol Timm only a short walk away. He peeked through the curtains and watched her vacuum and dusting, and fantasized over his plans.

He pulled on his shirt and his trousers, covering his wife's underwear then hid a 12 inch chisel, a craft knife and several self-locking ties in his pocket. He crossed the street.

"When she answered the door I asked if I could borrow a tin opener." He said.

With a neighbourly smile, Carol greeted him then she turned. This was his chance. He stepped inside and with the chisel, struck her a violent blow across the back of her head. She dropped to the floor, semiconscious, blood pouring from a gaping wound. Mitchell locked the front door and closed the window blinds.

She was his prisoner. He was now in charge, dragging her by her ankles upstairs to the bedroom, dropping her limp body on the bed. He removed his own clothing and stripped down to his wife's then climbed onto the bed.

Carol opened her eyes to the terrifying sight of Mitchell on top and she fought for her life, struggling for her freedom. Mitchel had his hands around her neck as he carried out his evil act.

He left Carol dead on the bed and returned home, throwing his blood soaked clothes into the washing basket then writing out a suicide note. It would be too late when his wife read it. He intended to end his life.

He called into the local chemist's shop and purchased a bottle of Paracetamol and several cans of beer. He then called into Maureen's place of work and asked her for his car keys.

That evening she read his note and called the police.

"He seemed anxious, confused, upset about something, but refusing to give an explanation," she told the police when they called at her home and handed them the note.

The police were still at her home dealing with a potential missing person, when Paul Timm returned home to find his wife lying on the bed, dead, her clothes ripped apart, her blood soaked hands tied behind her back, leg`s bound together.

The police heard his screams across the road as he ran from the house, inconsolable.

Mitchell had driven into Cumbria and traced to a layby on the M6

"The most horrific aspect, is to imagine the terrible vision suffered by Carol when she regained consciousness" a detective said, shaking his head, "To open her eyes and see him dressed in women`s clothes."

The trial lasted nine days, the jury deliberating for only five hours before returning a verdict of guilty of murder. Mitchell received a life sentence.

Had it been in the 20th century, Mitchell would have hanged

*

My friend worked for Customs and Excise. He rang me. His job was to check holidaymakers returning into the UK and examine the contents of their luggage, "for excessive amounts of alcohol or cigarettes."

He told me he had seized several bottles of spirits from a flight and took them home. "I organised a BBQ inviting neighbours, friends and work mates to a free booze-up. The BBQ`s were a great success, bottles carried home by neighbours in wheelbarrows"

"Someone told my boss and the cops came to my house. I was arrested for theft…I thought it was okay." He admitted taking the bottles home and holding a BBQ.

"A policeman asked why I had not invited him to the booze up. They treat it as a joke."

Charged with theft, he would stand before the Judge of Newcastle Crown Court, his career threatened and prison looming.

I told him it was one of those cases where the Judge could take a very serious view, sentencing him to prison as a deterrent to others similarly employed. "The judge could make an example of you."

My friend was honest and a devoted family man, a wife, mortgage and two children to support.

He stood in the Dock of the crown Court, knowing that night may be the first of many be in a prison cell: his life, his career shattered.

The prosecution barrister began to relay the facts of the dishonesty, including neighbours wheeling booze home, but His Honour interjected. "I am curious. What happens to all those gallons and gallons of whisky seized by Customs."

"It is flushed down the drain, Your Honour. It ends up in the River Tyne."

His Honour, a connoisseur of whisky, was clearly flabbergasted at such waste.

"My God… All that good whisky poured into the Tyne… for the fishes."

The judge shook his head and lost interest, retorting. "Why wasn`t I invited to the BBQ?"

My friend lost his job, but he did not go to jail.

*

Anthony Brakspear, a Zimbabwean farmer, stepped off his flight at Newcastle airport and arrested. Four of his twenty-one packing cases held at the Nottingham Freight Depot. A search had uncovered three rifles and several rounds of ammunition.

Brakspear, a white millionaire gentleman farmer, was at Market Street Police Station where I offered him legal advice. Tall, lean, tanned and gentlemanly, he looked out of place in his expensive hand-stitched suit, in a cell.

He relayed his story: His family owned the world renowned Brakspear Brewery, with huge investments throughout Africa and Europe. Nearing retirement, he and his wife decided to fly to the UK to visit relatives, unaware Customs were checking their luggage.

They seized a small arsenal of weapons: a Kommando semi-automatic gun, a Webley and Scott revolver and an antique, Flintlock pistol, with 58 rounds of ammunition. Mr Brakspear admitted they belonged to him.

At Sunderland Magistrates' Court, he pleaded guilty. I mitigated the facts, explaining he did not know the weapons were in his luggage. "They had been packed, along with his clothes, by a member of his staff who thought, wrongly, on this occasion, he would need them for protection. In Mr Brakspear's country it is not unusual for him to face wild and dangerous animals or evil men intent on robbery; people who would not hesitate to kill. It was routine for his House-Boy always to pack the weapons whenever Mr Brakspear left the house," I told the magistrates'

"In South Africa" I explained, "guns are carried on every journey. They are part of one's apparel, an extension of his arm; for self-protection when travelling across barren countryside."

The Magistrates' were sympathetic, recognising his good character, his honest demeanour, but my plea for the return of his guns, particularly his precious antique flintlock pistol, ignored.

Chapter Twenty Two

I unloaded my court files onto the desk, pushing them to one corner. Kath would collect them, make dairy entries, write to each client and keep on top of appointments. The hub of my office, she kept the wheels running smoothly and in the right direction: irreplaceable.

I eased into my chair, studying the indictments on my wall, thinking how mistakes and missed opportunities could have devastating consequences. One mistake may have saved the life of Marie Hines, the daughter of a Magistrate.

The police arrested her partner Anthony Nicholson Davison, several times, putting him before the courts. The Crown Prosecution demanded his remand to prison, but Magistrates` disagreed, granting him bail, and the opportunity to kill.

Anthony Nicholson Davison brutally murdered Marie on the 28th day of June 1992 and only days after granting him his freedom for the fourth time.

He killed Marie in a violent, gruesome way, her death having all the hall- marks of the psychopath Thomas Wilson Mitchell.

They met and soon fell in love, but Marie did not know him. She thought they could share their lives together, happy and contented and raise a family. Davison was courteous and respectful. Marie gave birth to their son, but Marie`s mother, had reservations taking an instant dislike to him.

Davison became possessive and argumentative. He was violent although Marie tried to make their relationship work. She was also frightened of him. Maybe deep down she already knew he would never change and eventually she could take no more and left him to return home.

Marie was determined never to see him again. Their relationship was over and he was not welcome at her parent's house.

Davison had other ideas and called many times trying to get Marie to go home, mostly under the influence of drink, abusive and argumentative, banging and kicking at the door, threatening violence. Marie's parents called the police and Davison arrested. He appeared before Gateshead Magistrates' Court where the prosecution asked for his remand to prison. "We believe he will breach his bail conditions and he return to Marie's house."

Davison promised to stay away and the court accepted his word. He broke his promise to the court and was arrested.

Again he promised not to go to Marie's home, begging for his freedom. The Court agreed accepting his false promises but he returned to Marie's home, shouting vulgar abuse at her parents and head butting their front door, threatening violence as blood dripped freely from a head wound.

Marie and her parents were terrified. Mr Hines thought the court had let them down.

"He looked mad," Mrs Hines would tell the Crown Court, "It was frightening. Like a scene from a horror movie."

Davison was a bomb about to explode but it seemed only Marie and her parents understood the danger they faced as their pleadings to lock him up went unheard.

The police were sympathetic promising to 'keep an eye' out. Her parents thought Marie was now safe and took a short holiday abroad but, within days, Davison brutally murdered Marie.

The Superintendent disclosed the facts and I noted the several opportunities missed to protect her, noting particularly the sequence of events:

April 18th 1992, Davison broke the window at Marie's parents' home. He arrested and bailed by the police.

April 19th 1992, Davison broke two windows at the house and assaulted Marie's mother, Mr Hines fighting him off with a stick. Davison arrested and held in custody for court.

April 21st 1992, Davison bailed by South Tyneside Magistrates' Court with conditions to stay away from the Hines family home.

May 26th 1992, Davison returned to the house and broke a window. He assaulted a Police Officer.

Gateshead Magistrates' bailed him.

June 13th 1992, Davison returned to the house and arrested for breaching his bail conditions.

Gateshead Magistrates' remanded him into custody for one week. Marie felt safe but, on his return to Court on 19th June, he was released to live with his parents and to stay away from the Hines family home.

June 28th 1992, Davison strangled Marie to death at their former home in Salem Street, Jarrow: the home they had shared with their one year`s old son.

The Superintendent relayed the horror of the incident: "He attacked Marie, tying the cord of a dressing-gown around her neck then beating her violently about the head and strangling her with his bare hands."

Mr and Mrs Hines were on holiday when they received the news and flew back to their worst nightmare. Marie was dead.

"When we went to see her at the undertakers we could not recognise her, she was so badly beaten" Mrs Hines told the local press. Mr Hines beyond despair, hitting out at the Court`s for granting him bail and demanding a change to the law. "This must never happen again."

Doctor James Sunter, the Home Office Pathologist, confirmed Marie`s death was due to a violent beating, strangulation and sexual abuse.

I visited Davison at Durham Prison, spending many hours taking his instructions, trying to understand what made him do such a thing: how his mind worked. Why he had so brutally murdered the woman he told me, he loved.

I sent a team of psychiatrists to the prison. They spent hours preparing their expert reports for the Court. My legal team required confirmation he was fit to plead.

Davison received a life sentence but then, from behind bars, he demanded custody of his son now two years of age. He was granted free legal aid to pursue his claim.

Mr and Mrs Hines would now face another trauma: the fight for their grandson, and they would have to pay all there own legal fees.

They had a stroke of good fortune. Lucy Winskill, a distinguished and eminent family lawyer, agreed to help. She battled for two years to secure an Order for custody.

"How could we allow this monster to get access to our grandson?" Mr Hines told the press as he went on a pilgrimage, seeking protection for all parents in a similar situation, moving tirelessly to form the Campaign for Rights for the Family and being assisted by the London based, Justice For Victim's Pressure Group.

He met Michael Howard, Home Secretary, and from his tireless effort's the Victim Support scheme implemented which, to this day, operates in every Court throughout the England and Wales, compelling magistrates' and Judges' to consider the personal statement of families of victims before sentencing the offender.

Mr Hines also took part in a BBC crime limited documentary. "All these things are very important and would tip the scales of justice back towards the victim, instead of the offender."

Mr Hines continues to be a monument to justice.

*

I had a variety of crimes to defend: murder, rape, robbery and a host of traffic offences added into the mix. I would represent Edward Carmichael Charlton at Ashington Magistrates' Court for driving his battered old BMW along Ashington Main Street without displaying a tax disc. Not a serious offence, but he had been a thorn in the side of the cops for some time, having notched up an armful of convictions, and they were determined to catch him.

A retired colliery worker, in his middle sixties, wrinkled and illiterate, he was able to find temporary work as a labourer on local building sites.

"I am pleading not guilty, Mr Gibson," The circumstance of his arrest had already been splashed over the front page of the local press.

Charlton was stopped driving his car, the officer painstakingly checking for minor road traffic offences, determined to "have him."

"He wanted to check my tax disc," he told me. "It expired months earlier." Eddie asked to hand the tax dis over but instead he popped it in his mouth, chewing and then swallowed.

"Where`s your evidence?" he laughed. "Prove it copper."

The Officer called into Court to give evidence: "I saw the road fund licence on his car. It had expired," He conceded he had no tax disc to produce as evidence and Eddie acquitted. The local paper took pictures of Eddie pretending to eat his tax disc, two of his arthritic fingers held high in solute to his success.

Months later, I discovered another side to Eddie Charlton. He harboured sexual desires toward elderly women, the older, the larger her breasts the better.

Work on building sites was limited so he looked for gardening work around the street`s professing to be an experienced landscape gardener, offering to cut lawns, clear weeds and dig ditches for a few quid, his ulterior motive to gain entry to the lady`s house and then to molest her.

Incredibly, he got away with it many times without complaint, until the daughter of one victim caught him in the act and the game was up. Several more victims came forward as the news spread and Eddie stood before the District Judge.

He pleaded not guilty and ran the defence of consent: "they agreed. They let me do it."

Two elderly women gave evidence, their account honest and truthful.

"Yes, he was a nice man." they accepted.

"Yes, I invited him in for a cup of tea. But not to touch me like that"

Eddie`s turn now to give his evidence and a woman Barrister would cross-examine him.

"You assaulted each of these women," the Barrister insisted.

"Aye, I played with their tits… a' give them a big slobbery kiss, but they said it was al'reet…well they didn't stop is." He told the District Judge.

"You pressurised them." Counsel insisted. "You forced yourself on them."

"Na…I didn't"

"You did"

"Didn't,"

Eddie lost his temper. "You weren't there. How the fuck d' ye kna'?"

The District Judge interjected, warning Eddie not to swear and answer the questions.

Our case was going the way I expected, downhill fast, evidence mounting by the minute.

It would be a question of the length of his sentence but Eddie continued to fluster and bluster, losing his temper and making a poor witness.

The Judge did not believe a word Eddie said then a question from the Barrister caused the court to erupted, into hysterics, when Eddie answered the next question from the Barrister.

"You parked your car about five hundred yards away from the lady's house. Why did you not park outside her house? Was it because you did not want anyone to know you were there, molesting her?"

Eddie was agitated, "I parked me car doon the street 'cause there was a line of fucking bollocks outside her hoose."

Eddie meant there was a line of bollards outside of the woman's house preventing him from parking there and tears rolled down Counsel's face, unable to continue her cross examination.

Eddie was convicted and placed on the Sex Offender's Register but he would not be going to jail.

The Court required him to report to the Police once a week and notify any change of his circumstances.

"Nor shall you go near a female of any age, unsupervised." The District Judge announced and Eddie`s lucrative gardening work had come to an end.

"How am a` to earn a livin cuttin grass and diggin gardins?" he protested.

"Take someone with you," The Magistrate responded: "or go to jail."

Chapter Twenty Three

The 18th century jurist, William Blackstone, said about our criminal legal system "It is better ten guilty person's escape than that one innocent suffer. A hundred guilty men go free than one innocent man convicted," A notable quote indeed, but has it stood firm in the 21st century? Sadly, it has failed miserably. I only have to refer to the Birmingham Five, the Guildford four, the Hillsborough Disaster and many more lying in their graves with a belated pardon.

Our standard of proof in the criminal court is beyond reasonable doubt. The jury must be sure, before reaching their verdict of guilty. In Scotland, the jury have the opportunity to chicken out and return a third verdict of "not proven," a kind of half- way house when the jury are unable to make up their mind but don't want the defendant to walk away completely free and with many suspicious finger's pointing his way.

Amongst English lawyers our legal system also allows the jury to make demands on the presiding Judge in what is known as a special verdict. The jury pronounce their finding on the facts then 'Pray the advice of the Court'.

The judge applies the law to the jury's proven facts and gives his verdict.

But for many years, certainly until the 1960's, our legal system began at the door of the court. As a Policeman, I was empowered to question suspect's anywhere and everywhere. In the back of my police car, in a pub or factory and could even question a child at school in the presence of his teacher. There were no restrictions: no limitations. Justice began where I decided and usually on arrest, not at the door of the court. Solicitor's entering the legal arena only after the suspect's admissions were signed and sealed.

A Policeman could spend hours interviewing suspects and without pen touching paper. Usually after the suspect had been left in his cell overnight and any denial's ignored as irrelevant, the route to obtain his admission unquestioned.

A great deal of trust was extended by the courts to the Police Officer, the veracity of his evidence rarely challenged.

One defendant told the Court he made admissions, only after "his head was flushed down the cell toilet" The court did not believe him and he convicted. The officer convinced the court he would have to have very long arms, as the loo flush button was located outside the cell door. He omitted to mention his colleague was outside pressing the button.

A defendant told the Court his admissions were made with both arms tied to the bumper bar of a VW car. Again, the jury convicted, although we shall never know the truth, but I do recall visiting that same police station and seeing a VW Beetle bumper bar lying abandoned in the corner of the CID office.

A Magistrate told me, "If a policeman tells me on oath he witnessed something, then it must be true. I will always accept his evidence, to do otherwise could cause anarchy."

"That may be so," I replied, "but each case must be considered on merit." I do not think he listened.

An entry in a police officer's pocket note book, not signed by the defendant as confirmation of his admission was always evidence relied upon by the court as sufficient to convict, even though the entry logged may have been weeks, even months, after the event.

Defence solicitor's found challenge to the officer's account almost impossible as conviction's frequently hung on the word of the Officer, and with no independent, corroborating, evidence.

There had to be change in the procedure, solicitors able to demand presence at Police Stations before the suspect questioned, ensuring, as far as possible, fair play and a recording of every word.

Codes of Practice were introduced demanding openness and full disclosure, warts and all, with all the inherent weaknesses on view. Nothing concealed, no information suspiciously lost, no matter how immaterial to the prosecution case.

Suspects interviewed at a police station and in the presence of his solicitor, the tape recording available for all parties and the jury.

In a stroke, justice began at the time of arrest, before the police interrogation. Questions in the police car on route to the Police Station deemed illegal and inadmissible. For the first time a solicitor was able to flex his legal muscles to challenge intimidation, threats and oppression and the suspect's salvation; his right to silence.

"If I don't answer your questions copper, you cannot convict me."

Convictions and justice much harder to achieve. The pendulum swung in favour of the guilty.

The legal protections introduced to achieve fairness swung in favour of the criminal… and a switched on lawyer. An impenetrable shield had developed. The law had to change.

The suspect warned he should answer questions. His refusing to give an account could place him in jeopardy of a conviction when an inference was drawn.

"The innocent have nothing to hide" our court's resolved, "Silence will no longer rule our courts."

Previous convictions of the defendant made admissible along with Special Measures and hearsay. A child or a weak- minded witness able to give evidence on video or from behind a screen

Expert's reports, i.e., medical or forensic, produced to the other side and no longer 'binned' or hidden if unhelpful.

Agents attending suspect's must satisfy minimum standards of legal competency. No longer would a 16 year's old girl be sent to represent a murder suspect.

Murderers acquitted may be tried again by the jury.

But still there is the issue of the advocate's competency.

How many times have the jury returned their verdict based purely on oratory skills of the advocate? Could an advocate's legal skills confuse or abuse the jury? The acquittal of Ronald Storey may be a good example.

Where experts disagree with each other`s conclusions, or the evidence complex or confusing, how can we allow a jury of people of average intellect decide? How can they draw a conclusion?

Is the jury capable of unravelling complex fraud and accounting procedures?

Is it time for the expert`s evidence to be heard by a Judge alone?

Chapter Twenty Four

```
                    INDICTMENT                    No.  T9 30 70 3

The Crown Court at

THE QUEEN -v-   MICHAEL ANDREW SWEENEY


          charged as follows:-
Count 1
                         STATEMENT OF OFFENCE
MURDER
                         PARTICULARS OF OFFENCE
MICHAEL ANDREW SWEENEY on the 8th day of February 1993 murdered Leslie McDermott




                                              Officer of the Court
Form 5088
```

February 1993. Michael Andrew Sweeney arrested for murdering Leslie McDermott. Newspaper headlines filled the front pages with police officers on hands and knees combing a layby on the A1 south off the Granada Services, Birtley, Durham.

The incident began with a fight in Sweeney's front garden, in the village of Donwell, and ended with McDermott's dead body being dumped in the layby.

Sweeney, a bus driver, had caught McDermott burgling his home and grassed him to the police. McDermott spent time behind bars and wanted revenge. There had been several incidents of anger and threats by McDermott toward Sweeney culminating with him banging and kicking on Sweeney's door, threatening to give him a beating.

SLASHED TO DEATH

By MATT CASEY

A NORTH-EAST teenager was stabbed to death today and his body was dumped on a motorway slip road.

Police launched a murder inquiry after the gruesome discovery of the body of Leslie Richard McDermott, who had suffered multiple stab wounds.

A passing motorist found the victim on the side of the A195 slip road from the A1(M) just before 2am.

The horrifying discovery was made shortly after 18-year-old Mr McDermott was involved in an incident about two miles away, near his home in Oxford Avenue, Donwell Village, Washington. A man is helping police inquiries. As the murder inquiry got under way the slip road was cordoned off.

A police spokesman said Mr McDermott had been involved in an incident in the Oxford Avenue area.

Confirmed

The body was taken to Sunderland General Hospital, where a post mortem examination was carried out by Home Office pathologist Dr James Sunter.

A police spokesman said the examination had confirmed that Mr McDermott had died from stab wounds.

Turn to Page 3

● STABBING VICTIM — Leslie Richard McDermott

SHORTLY AFTER MIDNIGHT INCIDENT REPORTED IN OXFORD AVENUE
1.56am BODY FOUND BY A195 SOUTHBOUND SLIP ROAD TO A1

Teenager's body dumped on A1 slip road

● DAWN SEARCH — police looking for evidence at daybreak today on the A195 Washington slip road from the A1(M), where the body of a teenager with multiple stab wounds was found by a passing motorist

McDermott was breaking into Sweeney's van when Sweeney shouted to leave it alone. Sweeney armed himself with a knife and stood at his front door as McDermott approached. They fought on the front lawn. Sweeney pulled his knife and stabbed McDermott several times, inflicting gaping wounds. "He was dead in minutes" the Home Office Pathologist the Home Office pathologist said, "There were twenty seven stab wounds to his chest."

Neighbours heard McDermott's screams. They saw Sweeney struggling with McDermott to his van, pushing him inside. Sweeney drove off dumping him on the slip road. A passing motorist spotted the body and called the police.

The trial was presided over by His Honour Judge Angus Stroyan and lasted four days. My barrister, on this occasion John Milford QC eloquently summing up the defence.

"Sweeney is an ordinary, decent, law abiding young man, not looking for trouble. Trouble came to his door, over and over again, until eventually pushed too far. He killed when he completely lost his self- control."

The jury returned a verdict of manslaughter on the grounds of provocation and Sweeney received a sentence to five years in jail.

Another framed indictment hung on my office wall.

*

Friday the 25th august 1995. "Mother Beaten to Death," was the headlines in the Journal.

Jacqueline Jean Moore was brutally murdered at her Hadston flat in Amble above the shopping precinct. A single mother, 37 years of age, Jacqueline was described to the press by her mother as mentally impaired and requiring special needs.

"She was kind, harmless, but easily exploited," a neighbour said.

A slow learner and with a pronounced limp, Jacqueline was a frequent target for teenagers hounding her for cash to buy drugs and alcohol.

The search for her killer was on and Detective Superintendent John Fenwick, leading the investigation told the press, "Mrs Moore, who was only wearing a T-shirt at the time, had suffered numerous head and facial injuries, including about eleven blows to the left side of her head."

"They would have killed her virtually instantly," he said, "but, before that, she had been whipped with a rope-like weapon, sustaining numerous lash marks to her buttocks, leg's and inner thighs."

Stephen Cowell, 25years of age occupied the flat next door. He and a fifteen years old boy were charged with Jacqueline's murder and appeared before Bedlington Magistrates' Court. They were remanded in custody. I later represented the boy.

On October 1996, Cowell and the boy appeared before, Mr Justice Holland at Teesside Crown Court. The evidence against the boy based solely on the testimony of Cowell and His Lordship refused to allow the case to proceed to trial against him. The charge dropped. The boy would go home.

Cowell gave his evidence to the jury. He said he caught the boy having sex with Jacqueline and warned him they would have to kill her to stop her telling the boy's girlfriend.

"At that point it was only a joke," Cowell told the jury. He returned to his flat, took a hammer, a chisel and a knife from his tool kit then returned to kill her.

Cowell claimed he had mutilated Jacqueline with his knife and whipped her with a thin curtain wire, hitting her over the head with a steam iron. The Home Office Pathologist, Dr John McCarthy, disagreed with his evidence and the sequence of the attack. Psychiatrists said he was a psychopath. He wanted to kill someone for years.

Cowell changed his plea to guilty to manslaughter on the grounds of his diminished responsibility. Headlines in the Journal read: "Life for Psychopath."

*

Midday on the 24th December 1995 and Christmas revellers filled the streets of Newcastle. Francis George Kelly had been shot and lay dead in the middle of the road outside Macy's Bar in the Bigg Market.

Anne and I were shopping for staff Christmas booze when Detective Superintendent Goff Nicholson rang: "Bert, do you know where Stephen Rice is hiding?"

"No" I said, although I had represented Stephen many times, he was never violent.

"I've not heard from Steven for some time." I said. "You must suspect him of being involved in the shooting." I suggested but Goff would not be drawn.

"If you hear from him let me know, his life may be in danger"

Mid-afternoon Boxing Day, Stephen rang me his voice anxious, breathing rapid.

"I'm in trouble, Mr Gibson," he said, his voice breaking off. I heard crying in the background.

"I shot Francis Kelly," he told me, "but he shot at me first. I was just defending myself."

He relayed the incident: "My life is in danger. They are after me. They are going to kill me. I'm hiding out, can't tell you where I am right now but I will let you know when I want to hand myself in. I just want a few days with my wife and kids."

I telephoned the Incident Room Market Street. The Superintendent was not available. I left a message for him relaying the conversation.

"Let us know when he decides to hand himself in", the call-taker said, promising to pass my message to Superintendent Nicholson.

They would continue their search for Stephen: possibly tap my phone.

29th December and Stephen rang. "I will hand myself in soon. I just want a few more days with my family. I know I'm going to get a big sentence." We arranged to meet. I noted time and day then rang the Incident Room. I left details.

I would meet Steven in Beaconsfield Street, off Westgate Road. It could be dangerous for me and I needed police protection. They would stake out the area, ready to jump in. Seize the suspect. I felt reassured.

I knew the deceased's family: they wanted Stephen more than the Police. There was a score to settle. I did not want to be in the middle when it kicked off.

"I will only hand myself in if you take me" he insisted, "I don't want to be shot by the cops either."

The day arrived. I drove up Beaconsfield Street looking for the door, sneaking a glance at my watch. It was nearly 3pm. I was on time, my eye's peeled for cops hiding in back lanes, under dark shadows or behind parked cars, a sense of protection spurring me on.

I pulled up and let the engine idle, wishing Steven to appear, to run into my car and to get the hell out of their fast.

I looked down the street: "The cops are bloody good: well hidden." My finger's tapped nervously on the steering.

I waited.

I sounded my horn. Stephen waved me into the flat. I shook my head, mouthing, "not fucking likely," gesturing him to come out.

He waved again, urging me inside. I mouthing; "piss off, you come here." expecting the cops to jump out, gun's leading the way.

"Where are they?"

Stephen waved again, insisting I go into the flat. I cursed, grit my teeth, cut the engine, and ran up the stairs. The flat was full. Family and friend's tearfully embracing him, holding onto his arms, his hands.

I urgent him outside expecting someone to burst through the door at any moment, gun's blazing, reminding myself I had a wife and two kids back home.

I grabbed his arm and pushed him down the stairs to my car, looking for signals from the cops. Steven slipped into the front passenger seat, crouching low, trying to hide in the foot well.

"Get up," I shouted. "Sit properly in your seat and put your seat belt on." I wanted anyone intent on shooting him to know the difference between us. I did not want to be in the cross fire, or mistaken for him.

I pushed first gear and up to the top of the street, taking a left down Westgate Road, checking in my rear view mirror every few metres, searching for cops with guns.

'These lads are good' I thought, 'better than me when I was a copper`. Can`t see them

In the City Centre, I became a bus, cruising down the bus lanes and into Market Street, puzzled why the police had not stopped me. Stephen would be safer in their custody.

Pilgrim Street, I turned into the narrow Police Station Yard expecting cops to rush out and surround my car: nothing.

I set the handbrake, pulled my mobile and pressed numbers. An officer answered.

"I have Steven Rice with me." He sounded surprised. I wasn`t sure he knew who Steven Rice was or why we were pounding on the back door of the police station.

"Stephen is suspected of the murder of Francis Kelly." That got the desired effect and the door swung open. We marched into the custody suite, as several excitable detectives appeared in a loud hustle and bustle then Steven, unceremoniously, shoved into the detention cell.

I was annoyed when I discovered the cops had not kept me under observation. No one was hiding in back lanes. Someone had forgotten to log my message.

Stephen was questioned, his replies forming a major part of his defence.

The storey unfolded: There had been trouble between families. Brick`s thrown through Stephen`s windows. Steven built up a line of brick`s on his windowsill so that shots fired at his house did not get through to his family. This was serious stuff.

"My family were in danger," he told the police: "I was frightened to let my kids go to school. To protect them I had to leave my home, hide away."

Stephen had reported the several incidents to the police. They had a record of each one. They would make a difference during his trial.

"Why has this happened?" I asked.

"It`s all over a valuable antique fireplace" he said. "Someone, and I can`t say who, had it delivered to an address in the West End, then moved it to another house. It was valued over £5000. He did not pay for it. The cops kept observations. They followed my wife. They saw her go inside a house and searched it. They recovered the fireplace. My wife had led the cops to the house."

"What has all this got to do with you?" I asked.

"They couldn`t blame my wife. She is part of their family. They couldn`t hurt her, so they took it out on me. It started with threatening phone calls, then bricks through my windows and shots fired at my car; my home. My kids were in danger."

He would not tell the police where he had been hiding: they would charge him with harbouring a criminal.

"I was sick of hiding away," he told the police: "I got a semi-automatic, an old gun, my only protection. It was Boxing Day, my birthday, and I wanted to go out, to celebrate. I was sick of hiding away, unable to go to the shops, see my kids, so I tucked the gun down my pants and headed into town.

I went into Macey`s in the Bigg Market. It was packed, queue`s up the street. I hid in the far corner where I felt safe, stacks of people about. I thought they wouldn`t try anything in front of all these people"

He rubbed his arm: "I was stood in the corner, a drink in my hand, away from the door, shoulder to shoulder, packed like sardines. Kelly came through the door, pushing through the crowds, his gun pointing at me. He pulled the trigger. I heard the bang and felt a sting in my arm" He rubbed the top of his right shoulder.

"He nicked my shoulder" Stephen showed the police the small scabby cut now healing.

"I drew my gun and fired. I was terrified: I didn`t aim. He staggered backwards in to the street." Kelly was on his back, motionless.

"I didn`t want this to happen" Stephen was in tears. "I never meant to harm him"

"Only two shots went off. He said, "He fell on the road. He didn`t get up. I think he was dead, I`m not sure. People were running about all over the place, screaming. I ran outside, dropped the gun. Just let it fall out of my hand. I think a Doorman picked it up."

Mr Justice Moreland, at Durham Crown Court would hear the case.

The Prosecution accepted shots had been fired at Stephen's house, the police report confirmed his family had been in danger. Stephen changed his children's school. He had changed the days of his community work so they could not find him. All this was in his favour. Stephen was lucky to be alive.

"But you had been utterly reckless, carrying a firearm in a public place," the Judge announced, handing Stephen an eight year's prison sentence for manslaughter and six years concurrent for possessing a firearm with intent to endanger life.

Chapter Twenty Five

I visited a twenty four year old on remand at Durham Prison. He was awaiting sentence. I needed instructions. We chatted about things happening in the West End of Newcastle. He called it a war zone. "it's the survivor of the fittest," he joked. It was never his fault. He would never accept blame every time he ended up in jail. Someone else was always responsible, even if he, as in this occasion, had been caught red handed with stolen goods in his hands.

I had sympathy for him. His mother had died of cancer when just a boy, his father abandoned him and his elder brother: both cared for by an aunt.

He had been through the legal system, the youth court and now he was in the big league, where criminals played hardball, honing his craft from others more experienced but similarly disposed, and building an unenviable list of convictions.

He boasted of his ability to burgle a house, any house, no matter how secure the alarm system, "even with the occupants asleep upstairs."

He told me he had case`d a large house in Jesmond, familiarising himself with their daily routine and soon learned they liked going to the theatre.

He bought two tickets and printed invitations, popped them through their letterbox. "I actually paid good money for those tickets," he smirked, "but it was worth it."

The invitation said they had won two tickets to the Theatre Royal and ended, "we hope you enjoy the show."

The couple returned from the theatre to find their home burgled and every stick of furniture, including the lounge carpet, stolen. "I knew where they would be and how long I had." He bragged.

"A pal helped me carry it away. I had a van on standby. The small items I got a taxi driver to put it in his boot. The cops never check taxi`s, no matter the time of night"

He rolled his own cigarette, took a long draw and blew smoke high into the air.

My visit was to discuss a burglary of a very large house in the Northumberland countryside.

"Aye, I was stopped with the gear in the boot of the car. The cops got lucky" he puffed on his cigarette.

"Paintings, all original, mind you, and silverware." He was matter-of-fact about it.

"Some you win some you lose."

"I changed the plates on the car," he said with a protesting, tut. "The plates cost me money." He thought it a big game.

"My driver had flu. He cried off, so I screwed the house myself. He missed out on his cut,"

"You missed out as well," I said telling him he faced another prison sentence.

"Do it standing on my head" he bragged, "Got money stashed away when I get out" he dumped his cigarette into the ashtray, "I will stay away from houses for a while." He decided, sitting back in his chair, yawning. "Maybe get back to the one arm bandits," he thought, "I can earn a big lumper doing that."

He told me how he would super glue a foreign coin to a piece of thread. "It has to be the right size and the right weight" then drop it into the machine, teasing it like a yoyo, pulling it up then letting it drop, rubbing against the mechanism until the machine was empty. "Some machines carry over £100," he smiled, "I can clear one in five minutes."

It would be three years before he played again on those machines.

*

Court Five at Newcastle Magistrates' Court a large oblong room with windows the full length of the wall overlooking Market Street. It was a dull day in October and I had a trial in the afternoon. My client, tall and rugged, charged with shoplifting which he denied.

The lights in the Court were illuminated, the prosecutor made an application to protect his only witness, a shop assistant who saw him do it. He wanted her identity protected and asking for screens to prevent the defendant seeing her. "She is very nervous and worried he might come after her,"

I reminded the court the incident had no aggravating features, no raised voice or threats, but the prosecution, as usual, swayed the bench and screens brought in.

The trial began. The witness hidden behind the screen. My client made no attempt to interrupt the proceedings. He sat quietly disinterested, staring out of the window, the Chairman praising him for the way he had conducted himself. The magistrates' were about to retire to make their decision, when my client remarked, "I didn`t need to look behind the screen, I could see her in the reflection of the window."

The court lights had acted as mirror, reflecting the movements of everyone in the room, including the shop assistant.

They promptly retired, returning in minutes with a verdict of not guilty. I often wondered if the Courts inability to protect the witness had influenced their decision.

Chapter Twenty Six

A It was a sunny day when I stepped from Newcastle Magistrates' Court and bumped into, Ron Curry Custody Sergeant at the Market Street, Bridewell. He had finished his early shift, thrown his civvy jacket over his stripes and was hurrying home, an expression of relief on his tired face.

"Been buzzing in there, Bert, sixteen prisoner's for court this morning," he said.

We set off round the corner to the Fire Station on Pilgrim Street where Ron encountered a young man, scruffily dressed. "Hey copper d' ye naa the way ti' the magistrates' court?"

"Aye son…" Ron pointed to Market Street. "Follow the line of shite."

Ron beamed, pleased with his response, as if getting his own back for 23 years of dealing with lads like him.

We parted company at the top of Grey Street where I spotted Chief Inspector Joe Hewison walking up toward me. He and I have been friends for many years and I knew he had a wicked sense of humour and given the opportunity, likely to inflict embarrassment on any occasion so, as we drew closer, I moved to the edge of the footpath, peering into parked cars, pretending to act suspiciously as if about to steal one. We were face to face when I mused," now Joe. Don't embarrass me," which was a foolish thing to say as he grabbed my arm, twisting it up my back and, in a voice loud enough for everyone to hear shouted, "If I catch you stealing women's knickers from Bainbridge's again I'll lock you up."

Heads turned my way. I turned scarlet. Joe winked then he freed my arm wandering off.

*

Monday, 5th January 1998, I arrived back at my office mid- afternoon.

Louise, my young receptionist said, "There is a man in reception who would like to see you. He says it is very urgent. He doesn`t have an appointment but he says he knows you."

I settled my files on the desk and invited him into my office. A tall, well-groomed man rounded the door introducing himself as Mr Thomas Brown. I didn`t immediately recognise him.

"I know you from my sittings at North Tyneside Magistrates` Court," he said, shaking my hand.

"I am in a bit of bother and I need your help," a Magistrate: needing my help?

"I have been arrested and charged with handling stolen property." That was the last thing I had expected to hear from a magistrate. They were strictly vetting, procedures conducted by the Court`s Administration and only honest, trustworthy members of society appointed.

"I`m innocent" he insisted, reading the expression of surprise on my face. "People brought things to my house for me to buy. I did not know they were stolen."

The leading case of Regina v Ghosh, came to mind, "On the facts, would a reasonable man believe the defendant (magistrate) acted dishonestly. If the answer to that question was "No" he would be acquitted. If however, the reasonable man believed he was, on the facts, acting dishonestly, then the jury must take one further step and ask themselves: "Did the defendant act dishonestly, on the objective test, the jury putting themselves in the mind of defendant?" If they concluded he was not acting dishonestly (even though a reasonable man would think he was) they must acquit," another piece of legal tomfoolery.

"Why do you say the items were not stolen?"

"They never said they were," He replied, convinced he was innocent.

"Why were people bringing items to your door? I questioned. "How did they know you were in the business of buying them?"

"They were people I knew." He said.

"Had any of them appeared before you at the North Tyneside

Magistrates' Court?" a pointed question, but one I had to ask.

"Some did, yes." I could not believe what he said.

"Then you accept they were dishonest, but you allowed them to visit your home. You were not suspicious?" He shook his head.

"Why have you come to my office? Why travel from North Shields, where there are many competent lawyers nearer to your home?"

"A friend suggested you." He then mentioned the name of an active criminal I frequently represented. I was shocked he would know such a person or call him a friend.

He left my office and I agreed to meet him at court where I arranged to view the video of the incident. The evidence was overwhelming. The police had spent many nights watching Mr Brown opening his door to thieves who handed him stolen property in return for cash.

One thief arrested informed on Mr. Brown, to save his own skin. The police wired him and sent him back, recording their conversation and showing the magistrate accepting clothing, jewellery and perfumes still with their labels on and handed them cash in exchange.

Mr Brown, stubbornly, protested his innocence.

At Newcastle Crown Court, he pleaded not guilty, despite my barrister's advice, suggesting most items were seconds or rejects and he paid a fair price. The items totalled £800. He paid £145 for the lot.

Mr Brown's conversations were read to the court, the prosecution asking him why he had said, "don't tell the law, if he did not think he was honest?". Brown told the jury, "I was laughing when I made that comment. It was just a quip meant as a joke, there was nothing in it."

The jury did not see the funny side nor did they accept his account, returning a verdict of guilty of stealing and attempting to handle stolen goods.

His Honour, Judge David Hodson, said he had brought disgrace to the North Tyneside Bench. "As a Magistrate you were in a position of eminence in your community. With such honour goes responsibility. The public quite rightly expect the highest standards of honesty and probity in those who sit in judgement of their fellow citizens," and jailed him for 18 months.

The Lord Chancellor's Department confirmed removal of his name from the Bench.

*

September 1999. Work was rolling in. Anne and I took off for America, visiting Boston and Cheers Bar. What a disappointment. The bar and interior replaced with shelves full of souvenirs and collectables: nothing like the television series.

I hired a car and we took- off into the White Mountains of New England and then we headed for the Canadian border and the awe-inspiring Niagara Falls.

Too soon, the dream was over and we returned to England to face a crisis of unimaginable trauma.

Anne diagnosed with cancer.

We were facing the biggest fight of our lives and despite several months of debilitating chemotherapy followed by radiotherapy, we lost her, and everything I had live for and loved disintegrated. Jane, Paul and I were in emotional melt down struggling from one day to the next; devastated and heartbroken, a devoted couple, happily married for 34 years.

I couldn't comprehend life without Anne, a wonderful, loving, caring wife and a mother whose life had been cut tragically short.

For month's I rattled around in the empty house, long sleepless nights and no interest in anyone or anything. I gave up my practice in Grey Street and took only part time, agency work: Jane and Paul my reason to go on.

The Vicar of Ponteland, Michael Jackson, called at my home. We talked and he posed a question. "You and Anne had 34 wonderful years together. If you had known when you first met, her life would end in this tragic way, and you would suffer deep pain and loss, would you have still married her?"

I nodded realising I had been lucky to meet Anne and spend so many happy years with her.

I had more than most.

At the Magistrates' Court, client's sought me out, offering their sympathy. I was grateful for their kind words. Even villains have a heart.

*

1st April 2008 Graeme Duncan arrested for the murder of Ross Davison, 19 years of age.

Duncan would stand in the Dock with his two pals and co accused, Steven Gilbert and Kenneth Power.

My son Paul was leaving Barrister's Chambers to join the Crown Prosecution Service. Before he took up his new appointment, I instructed him for this last time as my junior Counsel. Paul Sloan QC. would lead the defence.

I had known Graeme Duncan since his school-boy days. As a youth, he had attacked and wounded a man striking him with a jagged piece of timber in his neck. The man was lucky to be alive.

I attended Graeme at the police station and represented him at Newcastle Magistrates' Court. There would be no application for bail. He would go to prison. There would be no trial. The charge of murder not contested.

Duncan told me what happened, but as he relayed the incident to me, he kept picking at a scab on the back of his hand, squeezing it and deliberately making it bleed, then rubbing the blood between his fingers.

"I like to see blood" he said, spreading the blood over his hands and wiping it on his shirt.

I would need a psychiatric report.

Graeme Duncan and Steven Gilbert had been roaming the dark streets of Byker and looking for something to steal. By chance they met Kenneth Power and they decided to, "see what they could find," wandering back streets until arriving at Grace Street, the home of Ross Davison.

Gilbert stood under the street lamp, keeping watch. Duncan and Power armed themselves with wooden batons, in slipping quietly up the yard to the back door

Ross and his girlfriend were inside chatting when the door burst open. They rushed in and clubbed him several times on his head, his girlfriend looking on terrified, then screaming hysterically for them to stop.

"We just intended stealing something," Duncan told me. "We were after anything we could get our hands on then scarper," he said. "We grabbed an Xbox and ran." He picked at the scab.

You murdered for an Xbox," I said. "Something you could buy from a second hand shop for £130."

At Newcastle Crown Court, Duncan, pleaded guilty to murder. Power demanded a trial telling the jury he only struck Davison twice on his legs, blaming Duncan for the fatal injuries.

It took five days for the jury to return a verdict of guilty.

Gilbert pleaded guilty to conspiracy to rob explaining: "I thought they went in to pinch something. I didn`t know they were going to kill him."

Duncan received 22 years. Power 24 years and Gilbert 10 years.

Paul joined the Crown Prosecution Service, working hard to send my clients to jail.

*

Summer of 2013 and this railwayman`s son is now a grandfather and proud to have been a PC Plod but with no stab proof vest or pepper spray. No taser, Remington 870 shot gun, Walter, Glock or Heckler and Koch pistol.

My Dixon of Dock Green days had sadly gone. I turned in my truncheon to become a lawyer, but kept the police whistle I had blown on occasion to summon assistance from the public, happy respectful days.

Now –a- days, we have politicians fiddling Parliamentary expenses, bankers fiddling the accounts and industrialists polluting the environment. Nero fiddling while Rome burns.

Political correctness has reached levels of absurdity. The health and safety brigade have become farcical. The World Wide Web, a spider's nest of perverts preying on children. Teenager's obsessively texting and tuning into Facebook, MP3 Players and iPods.

Youngsters no longer go outside to kick a ball or play a game of British Bull Dog.

Our Health and Safety Executives outlawed it along with climbing trees, street cricket and Mount the Cuddy.

I still occasionally take off my golf sweater and spiked shoes to don my suit and tie and represent clients at police stations and in the Courts. My Law Society magazine reports that 1,600 solicitors' practices mainly dealing with criminal law may close. The government intended to supply legal aid to only 400 firms throughout England and Wales. Thankfully, they have seen the light and binned that idea. Jobs for now are safe.

For over thirty years, I fought for justice and fairness and I am proud that the Home Office saw fit to adopt some of my suggestions: authorising Custody Sergeants able to bail defendants with conditions. To appoint Queens' Solicitor's and the introduction of the Certificate of Readiness for all criminal trials.

Meanwhile you will find me sitting with my good friends, David Dick and Grenville Jones on a Wednesday evening at the Trinity Church, West Avenue, Gosforth, rehearsing with the Inspiration Choir and performing three times a year at The Sage, Gateshead.

We don't do any Bay City Rollers stuff, but I am trying to convince Gary Griffiths, our Music Director, I am up for a few solos – maybe, A Policeman's Lot Is Not A Happy One or what about, I Fought the Law and the Law Won.

My unforgettable Elvis impression, when I do Jail House Rock, will wow them – and I could always sing, Sue Me, from Guys and Dolls, for those people in the audience intent on dragging me to court to get their entrance money back.